THE BIG BOOK OF
KID'S ROOMS

D1296623

It's never been easier or more fun to turn your child's room into a place where imagination rules! With these eight all-new decorating themes, you can rustle-up a rustic bunk house for your favorite cowboy, or present a rosy palace to your sweet princess. If it's adventure your children crave, send them on safari in their own wild kingdom of exotic birds and friendly beasts. Or let youthful imaginations set sail on an ocean of nautical fun. They'll catch the joy of summer year-round with our cheerful bug collection. And check out the colorful Chicken Coop — it's a lively roost for recreation. Our step-by-step instructions will help you create these and other exciting rooms for the special kids in your life!

TABLE OF CONTENTS

SEP 1 1 2001

LEISURE ARTS, INC.
Little Rock, Arkansas

Portage County District Library
10482 South Street
Garrettsville, OH 44231-1116

BUG OFF!

Hide the fly swatters and throw out the bug spray — you'll want to make these cute critters feel right at home! With our easy instructions, you'll soon have a summer-bright swarm of darling dragonflies and lovable ladybugs, starting with this just-for-fun **Flamboyant Bug**. Instructions begin on page 8.

Purchased bed linens invite a hospitable hive of insects to drop by for a sleep-over on our **Creepin' Crawlin' Comforter and Shams**. Even the cushy **Ladybug, Dragonfly,** and **Butterfly Pillows** will welcome a hug. Don't worry, no insects were harmed to make this twinkling **Jar Of Fireflies Night Light** — it's a string of holiday lights in an old canning jar! And with just a little encouragement from you, the **Bug Tacks** will stick around to keep track of important notes on the bright **Bug-Catcher Bulletin Board**.

Even screens can't keep these friendly insects away, so propose an open-door policy with this new **Screen-Door Room Divider**. Use the **Bug Tacks**, shown on page 5, to hold a simple valance, then check out the cool **Biologist's Chair** and **Snug-As-A-Bug Rug**. Finally, top it all off with the **"Don't Bug Me" Sign** to repel pesky visitors. Your favorite youngster will get a "buzz" out of this new bug collection — and so will you!

FLAMBOYANT BUG

(Photo, pg. 2)

SUPPLIES

You will need one 3$\frac{1}{2}$" papier-mâché ball (for head) and one 4" papier-mâché ball (for thorax); 5$\frac{1}{2}$"h papier-mâché egg (for abdomen); 18-gauge paper-wrapped stem wire; 18" length of floral wire; wire cutters; four orange bump chenille stems; ten yellow chenille stems; two 1" dia. wooden buttons; two $\frac{1}{4}$" dia. purple buttons; pinking shears; two 8" squares of fabric for wings; one 10" square of fabric for wing spots; paper-backed fusible web; heavy-weight fusible interfacing; four straight pins; yellow, orange, light purple, purple, green, and dark green acrylic paint; non-toxic spray sealer; 1" stencil brush; drawing compass; craft knife; cutting mat; tracing paper; and a glue gun.

INSTRUCTIONS

1. Use craft knife to cut a $\frac{1}{8}$" dia. hole in head and in large end of abdomen. Cut two $\frac{1}{8}$" dia. holes (one on each end) in thorax. Cut floral wire in half. Glue one wire inside hole in head. Glue remaining wire inside hole in abdomen. Glue free ends of wires inside holes in thorax.
2. Cut six 10" lengths of paper-wrapped stem wire for legs. Cut three holes in both sides of thorax. Glue 1" of each leg in holes. To shape each leg, bend at 1" and 5" intervals from free end.
3. Paint legs and body green. Paint assorted colors of $\frac{1}{2}$" dia. dots on top of thorax. Paint small dark green dots around large dots. Paint 1" dia. buttons yellow; dot edges with purple. Use stencil brush to paint light purple stripes around abdomen. Apply sealer to bug.
4. Wrap and glue one length of yellow chenille stem around each foot. Cut two yellow stems into 4" lengths; glue one length around each leg at body. For antennae, cut two 7" lengths from remaining yellow stems. Curl one end of each stem. Wrap remaining ends around themselves and glue wrapped ends to head.
5. Glue small buttons to large buttons. Glue large buttons to head for eyes.
6. Cut three orange chenille stems in half. Wrap and glue one half around each "knee." Cut one bump from remaining chenille stem. Cut a small hole in front of head for mouth. Curl bump and glue free end in hole.
7. Omitting body and extending lines to connect wings into one piece, trace butterfly wings from large butterfly pattern, pg. 13, onto tracing paper; cut out.
8. Fuse interfacing to wrong side of wing fabric. Draw around wing pattern on wrong side of wing fabric; cut out. Fuse web to interfaced side of remaining wing fabric. Cut a second wing from wing fabric; fuse wings together.
9. Fuse web to wrong side of fabric for wing spots. Use drawing compass to draw eight 2" dia. circles on paper backing. Use pinking shears to cut out circles; fuse to wings. Pin wings to thorax.

BIOLOGIST'S CHAIR AND SNUG-AS-A-BUG RUG

Chair

(Photo, pg. 6)

SUPPLIES

You will need a folding director's chair with removable canvas back and seat, tracing paper, transfer paper, desired colors of acrylic paint, and a black medium-point permanent marker.

INSTRUCTIONS

1. Remove back and seat from chair.
2. Read **Transferring Patterns**, pg. 111. Omitting dotted lines, transfer insect patterns, pgs. 12 - 15, to fronts of rug, chair back, and seat.
3. Allowing paint to dry after each application, paint insects, adding spots and stripes as desired. Draw over transferred lines with marker.
4. Replace chair back and seat.

Rug

(Photo, pg. 6)

SUPPLIES

You will need a jute rug, fabric to cover edges of rug, glue gun, tracing paper, transfer paper, desired colors of acrylic paint, and a black medium-point permanent marker.

INSTRUCTIONS

1. Cut four 5"w strips of fabric in lengths to fit rug plus 1". Press all edges of strips $\frac{1}{2}$" to wrong side. Fold strips in half lengthwise with wrong sides together. On two opposite sides of rug, center rug in folds of strips; glue to secure. Center rug in folds of remaining strips. On top side of rug, fold corners of short ends of strips to wrong side, creating a mitered-look corner; glue strips to secure.
2. Follow Steps 2 and 3 of chair instructions to paint bugs on rug.

CREEPIN' CRAWLIN' COMFORTER AND SHAMS

(Photo, pg. 4)

SUPPLIES
You will need a purchased comforter and shams, medium-weight plaid and light-weight polka-dot fabrics for bug wings, paper-backed fusible web, embroidery floss, embroidery needle, 5mm chenille stems, assorted wooden beads for insect bodies, 3mm E-beads for antennae, tracing paper, craft glue, and safety pins (optional).

INSTRUCTIONS
1. Omitting bodies and extending lines to connect wings into one piece, trace wings of dragonfly and small butterfly patterns, pgs. 12 and 14, onto tracing paper; cut out. For ladybug body, trace entire outer line of ladybug pattern, pg. 15, onto tracing paper; cut out. For ladybug wings, trace only wings onto tracing paper; cut out.
2. Fuse web to wrong side of polka-dot fabric. Draw around all wing patterns on paper side of fusible web; cut out.
3. Draw around ladybug body pattern on wrong side of plaid fabric; cut out. Fuse ladybug wings to body. Fuse dragonfly and butterfly wings to wrong side of plaid fabric; cut out.
4. Use three strands of floss to work **Running Stitches**, pg. 111, as indicated on patterns.
5. For ladybug antennae, cut a 3" length of chenille stem. Glue one E-bead to each end of antennae. Bend antennae in half and glue to wrong side of ladybug.
6. For dragonfly body, bend one chenille stem in half. Twist 1/2" of bend. Thread 3 1/2" of wooden beads over both stem ends. Curl ends to shape antennae. Glue wings to back of body.
7. For butterfly body, cut a 7" length of chenille stem. Bend stem in half. Thread 1 1/2" of wooden beads over one stem end. Place wings between stem ends with beads on right side of wings; twist ends of chenille stem together. Curl stem ends to shape antennae.
8. Repeat Steps 1 - 7 to create desired number of insects. Use safety pins or needle and thread to attach insects to comforter and shams (insects are not washable).

"DON'T BUG ME" SIGN

(Photo, pg. 6)

SUPPLIES
You will need a 6" x 14" wooden sign; primer; yellow, purple, and green acrylic paint; fine-grit sandpaper; non-toxic spray sealer; tracing paper; transfer paper; black fine-point and medium-point permanent markers; plaid and polka-dot fabrics for ladybug; embroidery floss; 3" piece of 5mm chenille stem for antennae; two 3mm E-beads; craft glue; and 14" of 1/4"w yellow grosgrain ribbon.

INSTRUCTIONS
1. Read **Preparing to Paint** and **Painting**, pg. 110, to paint sign yellow. Paint top of sign green. Paint purple stripes around border. Lightly sand front of sign.
2. Read **Transferring Patterns**, pg. 111. Transfer sign pattern, pg. 15, to sign. Paint letters yellow. Outline letters, bug shape, and purple stripes with medium-point marker. Outline letters and bug shape with fine-point marker. Apply sealer to sign.
3. Trace wings and entire outer line of ladybug pattern, pg. 15, separately onto tracing paper; cut out. Draw around patterns on wrong side of fabrics; cut out. Place wings on body. Use three strands of floss to work **Running Stitches**, pg. 111, as indicated on patterns.
4. Glue one E-bead to each end of antennae. Bend antennae in half and glue point to wrong side of ladybug. Glue ladybug to sign. Glue ribbon ends to back of sign for a hanger.

BUG TACKS

(Photo, pg. 5)

SUPPLIES

You will need assorted fabrics, fusible interfacing for dragonfly wings, 3³/₄"h wooden peg clothespins, craft drill, map pins, desired colors of acrylic paint, non-toxic spray sealer, desired colors of 5mm chenille stems, tracing paper, drawing compass, and craft glue.

INSTRUCTIONS

1. Drill a hole in each clothespin a little larger than the head of a map pin; glue pin in hole.
2. Paint clothespins, adding stripes or dots as desired. Apply sealer to clothespins.
3. For chenille stripes on dragonfly, wrap and glue chenille stem around clothespin. For chenille stripes on butterfly, cut chenille stem pieces to fit around front half of clothespin. Glue pieces to clothespin.
4. For antennae, cut 3" lengths of chenille stem. Bend pieces in half and glue points to tops of clothespins. Bend ends of chenille stems to shape antennae.
5. For wings on each butterfly, use compass to draw one 6" and one 5" dia. circle on wrong side of fabrics; cut out. Gather center of circles to shape wings. Slide wings between front and back of clothespin; glue in place.
6. For dragonfly wings, fuse interfacing to back of fabrics. Trace wings only of dragonfly pattern, pg. 12, onto tracing paper; cut out. Cut two wings from fabric. Glue wings to back of clothespin.

BUG-CATCHER BULLETIN BOARD

(Photo, pg. 5)

SUPPLIES

You will need a bulletin board with a wooden frame, fabric to cover board, ¹/₂"w grosgrain ribbon for border, purple acrylic paint, non-toxic spray sealer, and a glue gun.

INSTRUCTIONS

1. Remove board from frame. Paint frame purple. Apply sealer to frame.
2. Cut a piece of fabric same size as board. Glue fabric to edges of board. Glue lengths of ribbon along edges of board.
3. Replace board in frame.

LADYBUG PILLOW

(Photo, pg. 4)

SUPPLIES

You will need a 14" round pillow form, fabrics for body and wings, heavy-duty sewing thread, six 1¹/₂" dia. buttons, two ³/₄" dia. buttons, yarn, thumbtack, string, and fabric marking pen.

Note: Use a ¹/₂" seam allowance for all sewing unless otherwise indicated.

INSTRUCTIONS

1. Read **Cutting a Fabric Circle**, pg. 111, and use a 7¹/₂" measurement for string to cut two 15" dia. circles from fabric for body and two 15" dia. circles from fabric for wings.
2. Leaving an opening for turning, match right sides and sew body pieces together. Turn right side out. Insert pillow form in body; hand sew opening closed.
3. To shape head, use heavy-duty sewing thread and baste around pillow 4" from edge leaving long thread ends. Pull thread to gather neck; tie thread ends together to secure.
4. For each wing, fold one circle in half with right sides together. Cut off and discard 4" of folded circle (**Fig. 1**). Sew curved edges together; turn right side out and press. Baste ¹/₄" from open edges of wing. Pull thread ends to gather wing. Fold gathered edge under ¹/₂". Sew fold to body at neck.

Fig. 1

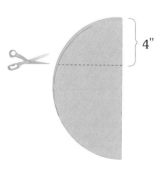

4"

5. Sew 1¹/₂" dia. buttons to wings and body. Sew ³/₄" dia. buttons to body for eyes. For antennae, thread a 9" length of yarn through pillow near eyes, leaving a 4" length of yarn at each end. Knot yarn ends next to head. Double knot ends of yarn.

DRAGONFLY PILLOW

(Photo, pg. 4)

SUPPLIES

You will need a 22" square of fabric for body, 1/3 yd of fabric for wings, polyester fiberfill, tracing paper, one 1/2" dia. button, two 3/4" dia. buttons, and yarn.

Note: Use a 1/2" seam allowance for all sewing.

INSTRUCTIONS

1. For body, match right sides and fold square of fabric in half. Stopping 1/2" from long raw edges, baste across short ends 1/4" from edge. Leaving an opening for turning, sew long edges together. Pull thread ends to gather short ends to 1 3/4"w. Sew over gathers to secure. Turn body right side out. Stuff with fiberfill. Sew opening closed.

2. Baste around body twice, making tail section larger than middle and head sections. Pull thread ends to gather. Tie thread ends together to secure.

3. Trace dragonfly wing pattern, pg. 14, onto tracing paper. Cut eight wings from wing fabric.

4. Leaving an opening for turning, sew two wings together. Turn right side out; press. Sew opening closed. Baste along straight edges of wings; pull thread ends to gather. Sew over gathers to secure. Repeat to make a total of four wings. Sew wings to body. Sew 1 1/2" dia. button to wings. Sew 3/4" dia. buttons to body for eyes.

5. For antennae, thread a 12" length of yarn through pillow near eyes, leaving a 4" length of yarn on either end. Knot yarn ends next to head. Double knot ends of yarn.

BUTTERFLY PILLOW

(Photo, pg. 4)

SUPPLIES

You will need a 22" square of fabric for body, 1/3 yd of fabric for wings, polyester fiberfill, tracing paper, two 1/2" dia. buttons, two 3/4" dia. buttons, and yarn.

Note: Match right sides and use a 1/2" seam allowance for all sewing unless otherwise indicated.

INSTRUCTIONS

1. For body, fold square of fabric in half. Stopping 1/2" from long raw edges, baste across short ends 1/4" from edge. Leaving an opening for turning, sew long edges together. Pull thread ends to gather short ends to 1 3/4"w. Sew over gathers to secure. Turn body right side out. Stuff with fiberfill. Sew opening closed.

2. Baste around body three times, making head and tail sections slightly smaller than center (body) sections. Pull thread ends to gather. Tie thread ends together to secure.

3. For wings, read **Tracing Patterns**, pg. 111. Trace butterfly wing pattern, pg. 12, onto tracing paper. Cut four wings from wing fabric.

4. Leaving an opening for turning, sew two wings together; turn right side out. Sew opening closed. Baste along straight edges of wings; pull thread ends to gather. Sew over gathers to secure. Repeat to make remaining wing. Sew wings to body. Sew 1 1/2" dia. buttons to wings. Sew 3/4" dia. buttons to body for eyes.

5. For antennae, thread a 12" length of yarn through pillow near eyes, leaving a 4" length of yarn on either end. Knot yarn ends next to head. Double knot ends of yarn.

JAR OF FIREFLIES NIGHT LIGHT

(Photo, pg. 5)

SUPPLIES

You will need an old-fashioned canning jar with a zinc lid, tin snips, and a twenty-bulb string of white mini-lights.

INSTRUCTIONS

1. Use snips to cut a 1/4"w slot in side of jar lid.
2. Place light portion of string in jar with plug end extending outside jar. With cord through slot in lid, partially twist lid onto jar.

SCREEN DOOR ROOM DIVIDER

(Photo, pg. 7)

SUPPLIES

You will need two 36"w wooden screen doors, 36"w shelf with brackets and hardware for mounting, three 2" (51mm) zinc hinges, three 3½" shaker pegs, primer, purple latex flat paint, orange and green acrylic paint, 1" dia. dot sponge, non-toxic brush-on sealer, painter's tape, newspaper, craft drill, wood glue, 2" lengths of craft wire, and all supplies listed under Bug Tacks, pg. 10, except map pins.

INSTRUCTIONS

1. Mask off screens with tape and newspaper. Read **Preparing to Paint** and **Painting**, pg. 110, to prime and paint doors, shelf, and pegs purple. Randomly sponge green dots over doors. Outline dots with orange.
2. Install shelf and brackets on first door. Drill holes along center of second door to fit pegs. Glue pegs in holes. Apply sealer to doors.
3. On door with shelf, install middle hinge 40" from bottom. Install remaining hinges 10" from top and bottom. Turn door with pegs upside down. Connect doors by installing hinges on door with pegs.
4. For insects to hang on screens, follow Steps 2 - 6 of Bug Tacks, pg. 10, to make insects. For hanger, glue one end of a wire length to back of each insect.

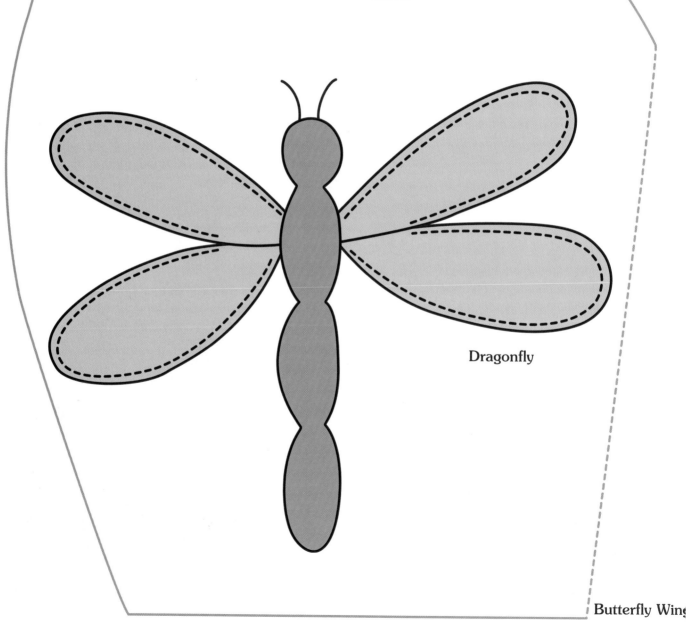

Dragonfly

Butterfly Wing

12

Inchworm

Large Butterfly

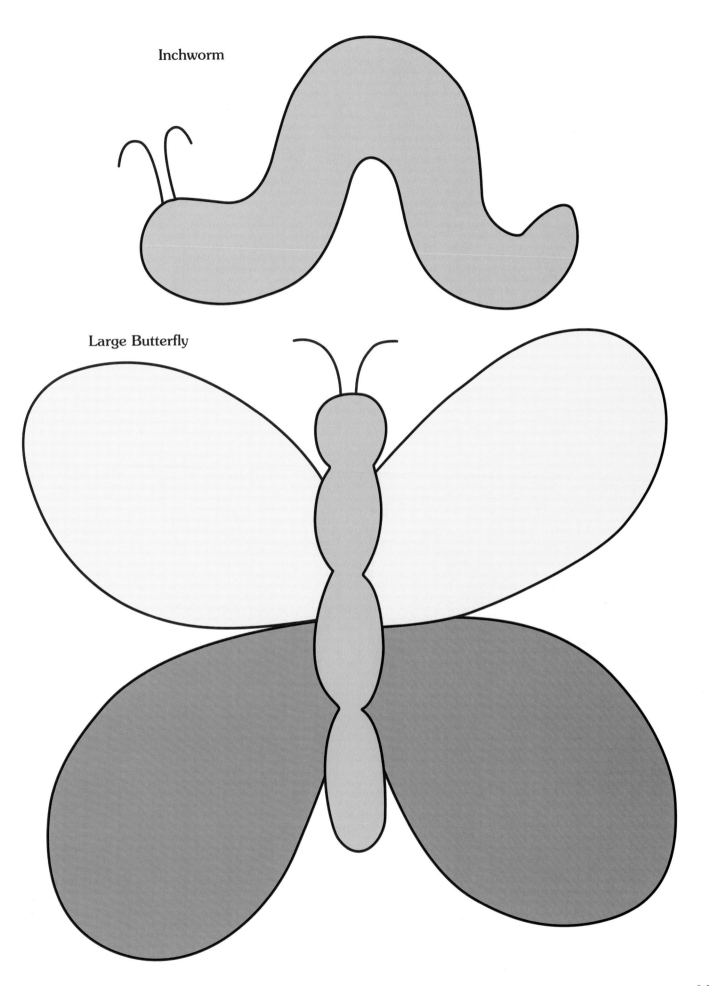

13

Dragonfly Wing

Small Butterfly

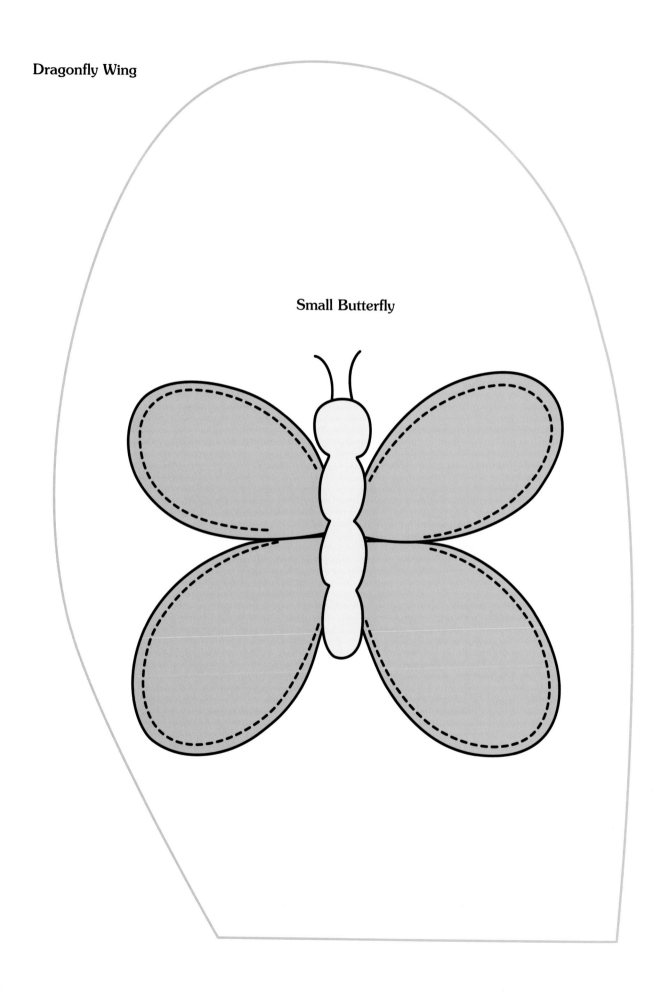

Sign

Don't ♥ Me!

Ladybug

home on the RANGE

Your best cowhand deserves this special place to bunk out! And these quick-to-rustle-up furnishings are a sure-fire pleaser for a busy trail boss, too. Mosey on over to page 22 to start your cowboy collection, including our rugged **Boot Lamp**.

A **Bandanna Valance** looks mighty nice paired with the oversize **Saddlebag Wall Hanging**. Western-theme pillows invite a weary ranch hand to rest a spell on the **Lazy ZZZ Bed**. Whether coonskin cap or ten-gallon hat, the **Hang 'Em High Peg Rack** can hold them all.

Keep photos of Wild West heroes close at hand in these **High Plains Photo Frames**. And if storage is a problem, you'll find the roomy **"Branded" Boot Chest** works great for holding all your buckaroo's gear.

At day's end, your little cowboy will snuggle under the warm **Saddle Blanket** and dream of new trails to blaze tomorrow.

(Photo, pg. 19)

SUPPLIES

You will need a twin-size wooden headboard, twin-size bed frame, drill, two 1" x 8" x 6½ft pieces of lumber for side rails, one 1" x 8" x 3½ft piece of lumber for foot rail, four 4" bolts with locking nuts, two 4" wood screws, six 3" wood screws, eight 5" long L-shaped brackets, twelve 1" long bolts with locking nuts, two 3" dia. x 5ft log posts, two 3" dia. x 3ft log posts, one 2" dia. x 41" log post for top of foot board, red flat latex paint, black acrylic paint, non-toxic brush-on sealer, foam brush, tracing paper, transfer paper, and any additional supplies listed in General Instructions (see Step 1).

Note: Drill pilot holes before using wood screws and bolts.

INSTRUCTIONS

1. Read **Preparing to Paint**, **Painting**, and **Transferring Patterns**, pgs. 110 and 111. **Do not** apply a primer before painting. Make a wash of red paint using two parts water to one part paint. Apply wash to headboard and lumber. Apply a second coat if needed for desired coverage.
2. Trace large brand patterns onto tracing paper. Transfer brands to top of headboard. Paint designs black. Apply sealer to headboard.

3. Follow manufacturer's instructions to attach bed frame to legs of headboard. Referring to **Fig. 1**, use 1" bolts to mount one L-bracket to each leg of headboard just above bed frame. With bottom edge of side rails 1" below bottom edge of bed frame, loosely bolt brackets to side rails. Mount a second L-bracket to each headboard leg and side rail 2" above each first bracket.

Fig. 1

4. Use 1" bolts to attach two L-brackets to each remaining end of side rails. Align foot rail with ends of side rails. Use 4" bolts to temporarily attach foot rail to side rails.
5. Measure from floor to top edge of side rail at headboard. Mark determined measurement on 3ft posts. Align top edge of foot rail with marks on 3ft posts. Bolt foot rail to posts (**Fig. 2**).

Fig. 2

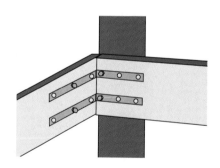

6. Use 4" wood screws to attach 41" post to 3ft posts above foot rail.
7. Working on back of headboard, use three 3" wood screws to attach each 5ft post to front of headboard. Hand tighten all bolts and screws.

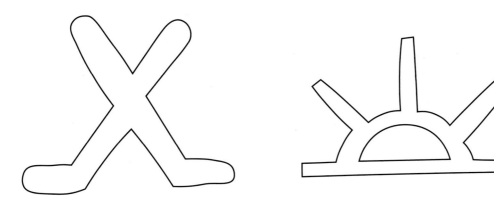

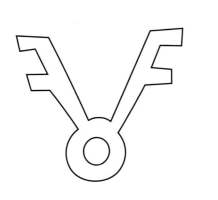

SADDLE BLANKET

(Photo, pg. 21)

SUPPLIES

You will need two 42" squares of plaid fabric for front and back of blanket, one 45" square of low-loft batting, $1/3$ yd of 42"w dark red fabric, $4^3/4$ yds of tan faux suede fringe, four $1^1/4$"w star-shaped conchos, four 14" lengths of tan leather lacing, one 20" square each of black fabric and paper-backed fusible web, black sewing thread, grey nylon thread, and tracing paper.

INSTRUCTIONS

1. Fuse web to wrong side of black fabric; do not remove paper backing. Read **Sizing Patterns**, pg. 110, to enlarge cowboy pattern to 18"w; cut out. Draw around pattern on paper backing; cut out appliqué. Remove paper backing and fuse appliqué to center of blanket front.

2. With nylon thread in needle and black thread in bobbin, use a narrow zig-zag stitch with a short stitch length on sewing machine to sew around edges of appliqué.

3. Cut four $2^1/2$" x 42" strips from dark red fabric. Press long edges of strips $1/4$" to wrong side. With strips placed $2^1/4$" from edges of front, topstitch one strip along each edge of front.

4. Place blanket front and back with right sides together and edges even. Center batting on wrong side of front. Using a $1/4$" seam allowance and leaving an opening for turning, sew front to back through all layers. Clip corners and turn right side out; sew opening closed.

5. With right sides together and beginning at one corner of blanket, match straight edge of fringe to edge of blanket front. Use a medium zig-zag stitch to sew fringe to blanket; press seam toward blanket back. Sew center of one lace to each intersection of brown strips. Thread ends of laces through conchos; knot to secure.

"BRANDED" BOOT CHEST

(Photo, pg. 20)

SUPPLIES

You will need a large solid wood chest, woodburning tool, red and black acrylic paint, wood-tone spray, non-toxic brush-on sealer, tracing paper, transfer paper, and masking tape.

INSTRUCTIONS

1. Read **Preparing to Paint**, **Painting**, and **Transferring Patterns**, pgs. 110 and 111. **Do not** apply a primer before painting. Make a wash of red paint using 2 parts water to 1 part paint. Mask off top and bottom borders of chest. Apply wash to lid and sides of chest. Apply a second coat if needed for desired coverage.

2. Trace cowboy and large brand patterns, pgs. 23 and 25, onto tracing paper. If desired, read **Sizing Patterns**, pg. 110, to enlarge or reduce patterns to fit chest. Transfer cowboy design to right end of top of lid. Reverse pattern; transfer cowboy design to left end. Paint cowboy designs black.

3. Transfer brands to top and bottom borders, repeating designs as necessary. Follow manufacturer's instructions to burn designs into borders. Lightly spray unpainted areas with wood-tone spray. Apply sealer to chest.

Cowboy

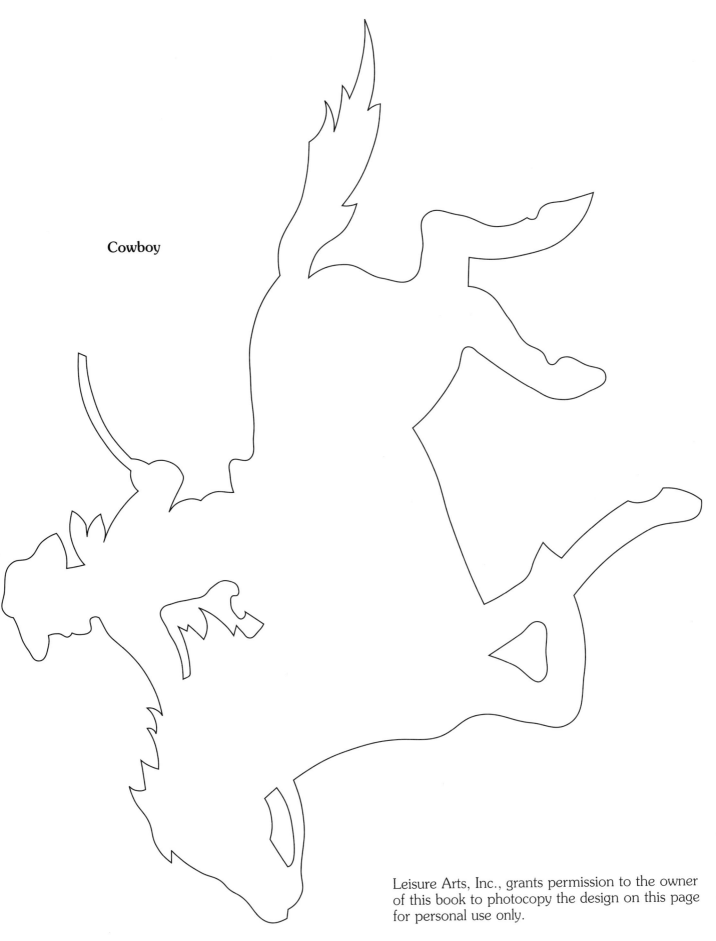

Leisure Arts, Inc., grants permission to the owner of this book to photocopy the design on this page for personal use only.

BOOT LAMP

(Photo, pg. 16)

SUPPLIES
You will need one pair of cowboy boots, 9" dia. shaped wooden clock face for base, lamp kit, self-adhesive shade kit, faux tan leather for shade, spool of red leather lacing, rotary hole punch, walnut wood stain spray, non-toxic spray sealer, $1/2$"w flat woven sisal, acrylic paint to match sisal, tack hammer, small finishing nails, decorative upholstery tacks, four 1" dia. wooden cap buttons, craft drill, four 2" long wood screws, and a glue gun.

INSTRUCTIONS
1. Follow manufacturer's directions to cover shade with faux suede. Spacing holes 1" apart, punch holes around top and bottom of shade 1" from wires. Thread lacing through holes; glue ends inside shade.
2. Glue wooden cap buttons to bottom of base. Apply stain to base. Apply sealer to base. Tack sisal around side of base, using tacks on points and finishing nails inside corners. Cover nail heads with paint.
3. Drill $1/2$" dia. hole through center of base. Follow manufacturer's instructions to assemble lamp on base.
4. Position boots on base; mark position. Drill four pilot holes through base and soles of boots (two screws for each boot). Screw boots to base. Place shade on lamp.

BANDANNA VALANCE

(Photo, pg. 18)

SUPPLIES
You will need a 45" square of cowboy print fabric, $2^3/4$ yds of faux suede fringe, four yds of rope, two 8" lengths of floral wire, and a glue gun.

INSTRUCTIONS
1. Matching wrong sides, fold fabric in half diagonally. With edges even, sew edges together to form a triangle. With 1" of fringe ends overlapping folded edge of fabric and folding fringe at corner as necessary, sew fringe to sewn edges.
2. Cut two 54" lengths of rope. Cut remaining length in half. Coil each long piece three times. Wrap one short length around each group of coils. Use wires to secure wraps. Glue wraps to back of coils. Thread ends of valance through coils.

HANG 'EM HIGH PEG RACK

(Photo, pg. 19)

SUPPLIES
You will need a wooden peg rack, red acrylic paint, wood-tone spray, non-toxic spray sealer, metal stars (we found ours at a flea market), $3/4$" long wood screws, screwdriver, and a woodburning tool.

INSTRUCTIONS
1. Read **Preparing to Paint** and **Painting**, pg. 110. **Do not** apply primer to peg rack. Make a wash of red paint using 2 parts water to 1 part paint. Paint top, sides, and bottom of rack with wash. Paint sides of pegs with wash.
2. Use a pencil to draw a dot and dash design around edges of rack. Draw star burst designs on ends of pegs. Follow tool manufacturer's instructions to woodburn drawn designs.
3. Apply wood-tone to peg rack. Apply sealer to peg rack. Screw stars to rack between pegs.

PINTO PILLOW

(Photo, pg. 19)

SUPPLIES

You will need an 11" square knife-edge pillow form, 8" square of print fabric, 1"w paper-backed fusible web tape, and 2½ yards of natural rope braid.

INSTRUCTIONS

1. Fuse web tape to wrong side of fabric along two opposite edges. Remove paper backing and press fused edges 1" to wrong side. Place form at center on wrong side of fabric piece. Bring pressed edges of fabric together over form; hand sew edges together to secure. Fold remaining ends of fabric into points. Overlap points at front of pillow; hand sew to secure.
2. Tie a knot 4" from each end of braid. Wrap braid around pillow and knot ends together on front.

BANDANNA FOLD PILLOW

(Photo, pg. 19)

SUPPLIES

You will need a 16" square knife-edge pillow form, 45" square of cowboy print fabric, 1"w fusible web tape, 2" dia. concho, 24" length of brown leather lace, and safety pins.

INSTRUCTIONS

1. Fold lace in half. Thread ends of lace through concho, pulling ends until concho is centered on lace. Pull ends of lace through loop to form a slide; set aside.
2. Fuse web tape to wrong side of fabric along two opposite edges. Remove paper backing and press fused edges 1" to wrong side. Repeat to hem two remaining sides.
3. Place form at center on wrong side of fabric. Bring two opposite sides over form; hand sew edges together to secure. Thread remaining fabric ends through the slide. Pull lace ends to tighten; tie lace ends in a knot. Tuck fabric ends under; hand sew to secure.

BOOT-SCOOTIN' BOLSTER

(Photo, pg. 19)

SUPPLIES

You will need batting, 30" square of boot print fabric, and two 36" lengths of natural rope braid.

INSTRUCTIONS

1. Fold and roll batting into a 15" long x 6" dia. cylinder.
2. Press one edge of fabric 1" to wrong side. On wrong side of fabric, center length of cylinder on edge opposite fold. Roll cylinder in fabric to pressed edge, covering batting in fabric. Hand sew pressed edge of fabric to secure.
3. Knot ends of braid. Gather fabric at ends of bolster; tie gathers with braid. Tuck fabric ends into gathers.

(Photo, pg. 20)

Boot Frame

SUPPLIES
You will need a photo frame with flat border, tan and brown acrylic paint, fine grit sandpaper, spray sealer, boot motif fabric, paper-backed fusible web, brown card stock, and a glue gun.

INSTRUCTIONS
1. Read **Preparing to Paint** and **Painting**, pg. 110. Paint frame brown, then tan. Lightly sand to remove tan paint in some areas.
2. On wrong side of fabric, fuse web over desired motif. Cut out motif; fuse to card stock. Glue cutout to frame. Apply sealer to frame.

Branded Frame

SUPPLIES
You will need a photo frame with flat border and rope hanger, tracing paper, transfer paper, and a woodburning tool.

INSTRUCTIONS
1. Trace small branding patterns. Transfer patterns to border of frame.
2. Follow manufacturer's instructions to burn brands into frame.

Small Brands

(photo, pg. 18)

SUPPLIES

You will need a 30" x 45" piece of pinto print fabric for back, 20¹/₂" x 45" piece of brown corduroy, four 4¹/₂" x 15¹/₂" pieces of light tan faux suede, two 7" x 44" strips of cowboy print fabric, pinking shears, two 2" dia. conchos, two 24" lengths of brown leather lacing, ¹/₂"w paper-backed fusible web tape, 7" dia. plate, fabric marking pen, and a 36" length of ³/₄" dia. dowel rod.

Note: Use a ¹/₄" seam allowance for all sewing unless otherwise indicated.

INSTRUCTIONS

1. On wrong side of fabric for back, fuse web tape along all edges. Fuse all edges ¹/₂" to wrong side. Matching wrong sides and short edges, fold pinto print fabric in half. For rod pocket, sew across fabric 1³/₄" from fold. Unfold fabric so that one bottom edge is nearest you. Fuse web tape to wrong side along outer edges below rod pocket. Refold fabric and fuse halves together.

2. For pockets, press one long edge of corduroy 5" to wrong side. Press remaining long edge 1¹/₂" to wrong side.

3. For flaps, use plate to draw round corners on one short end of each suede piece (**Fig. 1**). For each flap, place two suede pieces with right sides together. Leaving short straight edges open for turning, sew flap pieces together along three sides. Turn flaps right side out; press. To finish tops of flaps, trim open edges with pinking shears.

Fig. 1

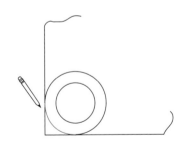

4. With top 4¹/₂" of flaps inside top edge of pocket, sew flaps to pocket near pinked edges (**Fig. 2**). Sew again near top edge of pocket. Fold flaps down. Sew a length of leather lace 2" above bottom center of each flap through flaps and front of pockets. Thread lace ends through conchos and knot to secure.

Fig. 2

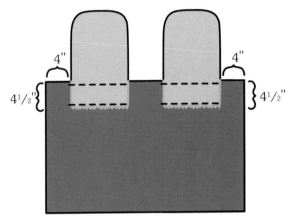

5. Fold pockets and back with short edges together to find centers on each long edge. Mark centers with pins. With wrong side bottom edge of pocket 1" from right side bottom edge of back, match centers and sew a vertical seam down center of pockets. Sew selvage edges of pockets to back 1" from edges of back. To shape pockets, make 1³/₄" tucks on both sides of each pocket; pin to secure. Sew bottom of pockets to back. Insert dowel rod into rod pocket.

6. For each tie, press long edges of one cowboy print strip ¹/₄" to wrong side. Match right sides and sew short edges together. With seam at center back, press ties flat. Press each end in opposite directions to form points. Repeat to make second tie. Knot ties on dowel rod.

good morning, PRINCESS

Satin roses, light-as-air tulle, and cascades of swirling ribbon set the scene for this soft and feminine room. Once upon a time, your little princess could have only dreamed of such a fairy-tale place. To make the **Ballerina Bunny** and other delightful projects, turn to page 36.

Embraced by petal-soft swags, the **Beribboned Window Topper** is secured with tributes of pink roses. More of the perfect posies bloom on the **Rosy Table Topper, Nosegay Jewelry Box**, and **Crown of Roses Lamp**. And each new day is made special with the sweet greetings painted on the **"Good Morning, Princess!" Dresser**.

She'll slumber happily ever after under this lovely **Canopy of Roses**, especially when cushioned with a delicate **Rose Pouf Pillow**. Satin ribbon blossoms are stitched on the ruffled spread and pillow sham to make a regal bed. And what prettier throne for the royal miss to sit upon than the beautiful **Princess Chair**?

(Photo on pg. 33)

SUPPLIES
You will need a wooden dresser with mirror; Kraft paper; masking tape; primer; white latex paint; non-toxic brush-on sealer; white, pink, dark pink, light purple, purple, light blue, blue, green, and dark green acrylic paint; tracing paper; and transfer paper.

1. Remove drawer pull hardware. Read **Preparing to Paint** and **Painting**, pg. 110. Use Kraft paper to mask off mirror glass. Paint dresser white.

2. Read **Painting Details**, **Sizing Patterns**, **Tracing Patterns**, and **Transferring Patterns**, pgs. 110 and 111. Transfer medium posy pattern, pg. 37, twice (once in reverse) to front of each drawer, crossing ribbon ends at drawer pull position. Transfer desired number of large posy, pg. 38, and ribbon half patterns, to top of dresser, reversing ribbon at one end and extending ribbons between posies. If desired, enlarge or reduce "Good Morning Princess" pattern. Transfer pattern to mirror frame above mirror. Paint designs. If desired, paint structural details of dresser pink.

3. Apply sealer to dresser. Replace drawer pulls.

Leisure Arts, Inc., grants permission to the owner of this book to photocopy the design on this page for personal use only.

Ribbon Half

Medium Posy

Small Posy

Large Posy

38

(Photo on pg. 34)

SUPPLIES

You will need a wooden chair; primer; white latex paint; white, pink, dark pink, light purple, purple, light blue, blue, green, and dark green acrylic paint; non-toxic brush-on sealer; tracing paper; transfer paper; $^1/_2$"w paper-backed fusible web tape; fabric to cover seat; sheer white fabric for underskirt; 45"w white tulle for skirt; pink artificial roses; $^3/_8$"w purple satin ribbon; $^1/_4$"w pink satin ribbon; staple gun; glue gun; and 1" thick foam to pad seat.

1. Read **Preparing to Paint**, **Painting**, **Painting Details**, **Tracing Patterns**, and **Transferring Patterns**, pgs. 110 and 111. Paint chair white. Transfer two ribbon half patterns (one in reverse), pg. 37, one large posy, and two small posy patterns, pg. 38, to chair back. Paint designs. Apply sealer to chair.
2. To pad chair, cut foam to fit seat. Place foam on wrong side of fabric. Cut out fabric 3" from edges of foam. Staple edges of foam to seat. Cover seat with fabric, stapling edges of fabric to sides of seat $^1/_2$" from top edge and clipping at corners as necessary. Trim fabric to within $^1/_2$" of staples.
3. For underskirt, measure around seat; multiply by 2. Measure from top edge of seat to floor; add $^1/_4$". Cut underskirt fabric the determined measurements. Fuse web tape along one long edge and both short edges on wrong side of underskirt. Remove paper backing. Fuse edges $^1/_2$" to wrong side. Baste $^1/_2$" from raw edge; pull thread ends to gather fabric to fit around chair with a 2" overlap. Beginning at back of chair, staple gathered underskirt around seat $^1/_2$" from top edge.
4. For skirt, measure around seat; multiply by 2.5. Measure from $^1/_2$" below seat to floor; multiply by 2. Cut tulle determined measurements. Fold tulle in half lengthwise. Baste $^1/_4$" from long raw edges. Pull thread ends, gathering tulle to fit around chair with a 2" overlap. Leaving two roses intact, clip petals from remaining roses. Place petals inside skirt, stitch ends closed. Staple skirt over underskirt $^1/_2$" from top edge of chair.
5. Glue a length of purple ribbon around seat to cover staples. Cut remaining roses from stems. Cut two 1 yd lengths from each color ribbon. Tie one of each color ribbon together into a double bow. Repeat with remaining 1 yd ribbon lengths. Glue bows and roses to corners of seat.

(Photo on pg. 30)

SUPPLIES

You will need a 20" tall stuffed toy bunny, 1 yd of small ribbon roses on a matching ribbon, three large ribbon roses, three 36" lengths of $^3/_8$"w purple satin ribbon, 48" of 1$^1/_4$"w pink satin ribbon, $^2/_3$ yd of 45"w pink tulle, and a glue gun.

1. For bunny's tutu, fold tulle in half twice, matching long edges. Baste through all layers along one long edge. Pull thread ends to gather tulle to 30". Center 1$^1/_4$"w ribbon on gathered edge. Topstitch ribbon to tulle. Cut fourteen small roses from ribbon; glue to tulle. Wrap tutu around bunny. Tie ribbon ends into a bow at front of bunny.
2. Glue a length of ribbon with roses around bunny's neck. Tie purple ribbons together in a bow around bunny's ears. Glue large roses to center of bow.

(Photo on pg. 32)

SUPPLIES

You will need one wooden candlestick lamp with approx. 9" dia. shade; artificial rose bushes; glue gun; primer; white, pink, and purple paint; non-toxic spray sealer; and $^1/_3$ yd of 45"w pink tulle.

1. Read **Preparing to Paint** and **Painting**, pg. 110. Paint lamp base. Apply sealer to lamp base.
2. Remove roses from bushes. Glue roses to lamp shade. Cut tulle into two 6" x 45" strips. Tie loose knots in strips at 6" intervals. Glue strips around top and bottom edges of shade, trimming to fit.

(Photo on pg. 35)

SUPPLIES
You will need a 12" round pillow form, 1 yd of white fabric, 1 yd of 45"w purple tulle, silk rose leaves, thumbtack, string, pencil, and a rubber band.

1. Read **Cutting a Fabric Circle**, pg. 111, and use a 15" measurement to cut a 30" circle for pillow cover from white fabric. Center pillow form on wrong side of cover. Gather cover around form and secure with a rubber band. Trim excess fabric.
2. Cut tulle into 6" x 44" strips. For rose center, cut a 12" length from one strip. Tie rose center into a loose knot. Sew rose center to pillow over rubber band.

3. To make "petals" on each remaining strip, gather strip across width at 4" intervals (**Fig. 1**). Sew each gather to secure. Beginning next to rose center and making petals looser as rose becomes wider, sew gathers to pillow. Continue until rose is 7" dia. Sew leaves to side of rose.

Fig. 1

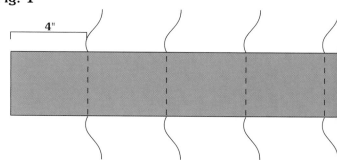

(Photo on pg. 32)

SUPPLIES
You will need pink medium-weight fabric, 45"w white tulle, two 48" lengths of 1¼"w pink satin ribbon, thumbtack, string, fabric marking pen, glue gun, and two silk roses.

1. Measure from center of table to floor; add 1½". Read **Cutting a Fabric Circle**, pg. 111, and use determined measurement to cut tablecloth from fabric. Repeat to cut a circle from tulle.

2. Press edges of tablecloth ½", then 1" to wrong side. Topstitch to secure.
3. Center tablecloth over table. Center tulle circle over tablecloth. Gather tulle at edge of tabletop. Sew gathers to tablecloth. Repeat, gathering tulle approx. 24" from first gather.
4. Tie ribbon lengths into bows. Sew bows to gathers. Cut roses from stems. Glue roses to bows.

(Photo on pg. 35)

SUPPLIES
You will need an adjustable-width curved continental curtain rod, 20 yds of 45"w white tulle, large dark pink roses, medium light pink roses, 10 yds each of assorted width pink and purple satin ribbons, white floral tape, white floral wire, wire cutters, 3"w white ribbon, and a glue gun.

1. Carefully bend rod to increase curve (we bent our curtain rod to 12" deep and 30"w). Cut four 5 yd lengths of tulle. Baste across one short edge of each panel. Pull thread ends to gather each panel to fit ¼ of length of rod. Glue gathered ends to back of rod. Flip panels to front of rod. Glue white ribbon to back of rod.

2. For each tie-back bouquet, trim stems of one large rose and five medium roses to 6". Tape roses together to form a bouquet. Wrap stems with a length of wire, leaving 4" of wire ends free. Cut four or five different length ribbons for each bouquet.
3. Clip petals from three medium roses. Cut remaining roses from stems. Glue roses to front of rod. Follow manufacturer's instructions to install rod on wall. Gather tulle as desired. Wrap wire ends of bouquets around gathers; fasten bouquets to wall as desired. Tuck petals into folds of panel swags.

Have no fear of the deadly tse-tse fly — the **"Mosquito Netting"** Window Treatment is handy to have hanging around while your intrepid explorer rests on an assortment of ferociously fun pillows.

To make the wild window seat cushion, just fold fabric around a foam piece and sew a few quick stitches. Take aim at the **Safari Nightstand** and **Zebra Rug**, too — they're so easy to make, you can't miss!

Discover our **Bamboo Headboard** and **Jungle Canopy**! This untamed setting begins with an ordinary headboard covered by raffia-tied canes — but look out! — hiding among those **Tasseled and Tied Pillows** is one fierce-looking **Lion Pillow** (he's really just an old softy on the inside). In case things get too wild, we can always hide behind the **Bamboo Screen**. Stenciled with palm trees and toucans, it's great camouflage for young adventurers.

BAMBOO LAMP

(Photo, pg. 42)

SUPPLIES

You will need a self-adhesive lampshade, cheetah-print tissue paper, black gimp, $1/8$"w brown suede lace, fine-point light green opaque marker, 3" dia. x 9"h snack chip can, hammer and nail, 8" dia. wood round, four 2" dia. wooden napkin rings, lamp kit with rod, $1^1/2$" piece of threaded rod, coupling for rod, primer, green acrylic paint, non-toxic spray sealer, glue gun, bamboo stakes, 9" x 10" piece of tan fabric, and a drill.

INSTRUCTIONS

1. Drill a $1/2$" dia. hole in center of wood round. Glue napkin rings to bottom of wood round for feet. Read **Preparing to Paint** and **Painting**, pg. 110, to prime and paint base.

2. For top of lamp, use hammer and nail to punch a $1/2$" hole in center of metal end of can. Use coupling to attach $1^1/2$" threaded rod to one end of lamp kit rod. Follow manufacturer's instructions to assemble lamp hardware with extended rod inside can and bulb socket on outside top of can.

3. Wrap and glue fabric around can. Cut bamboo stakes approx. $1/2$" longer than can. Glue stakes around can. Wrap two lengths of suede lace around bamboo and tie to secure.

4. Follow manufacturer's instructions to cover lampshade with tissue paper. Use green marker to outline cheetah spots. Apply sealer to lampshade; allow to dry. Glue gimp around edges of lampshade. Glue suede lace around gimp.

BAMBOO SCREEN

(Photo, pg. 47)

SUPPLIES

You will need a purchased bamboo screen with canvas panels; stencil plastic; craft knife; cutting mat; white, yellow, gold, orange, brown, purple, light green, green, and black acrylic paint; stencil brush; stencil adhesive; and black fine-point and medium-point permanent markers.

Note: You may wish to practice painting stencils on paper before painting on screen. Allow paint to dry before changing stencils.

INSTRUCTIONS

1. Use fine-point marker for all tracing. Trace toucan body, beak, tree trunk, leaves, and leaf shading separately onto pieces of stencil plastic. Use craft knife to cut out centers of stencils. Apply adhesive to wrong sides of stencils.

2. Smooth stencils onto screen as desired. Using an up-and-down motion and a nearly dry brush, paint tree trunk gold and shade edges with brown. Paint leaves light green and shade with green. Paint toucan purple and beak orange. Paint a white dot for toucan's eye. Paint a black dot in center of white dot. Paint a yellow stripe on beak. Repeat to paint desired number of stencils.

3. Clean stencils with soapy water; allow to dry. Turn stencils over to reverse the design. Repeat Step 2 to paint desired number of reversed stencils.

4. Use fine-point marker to add veins to leaves and wavy lines to trunks. Use medium-point marker to draw feet under toucans.

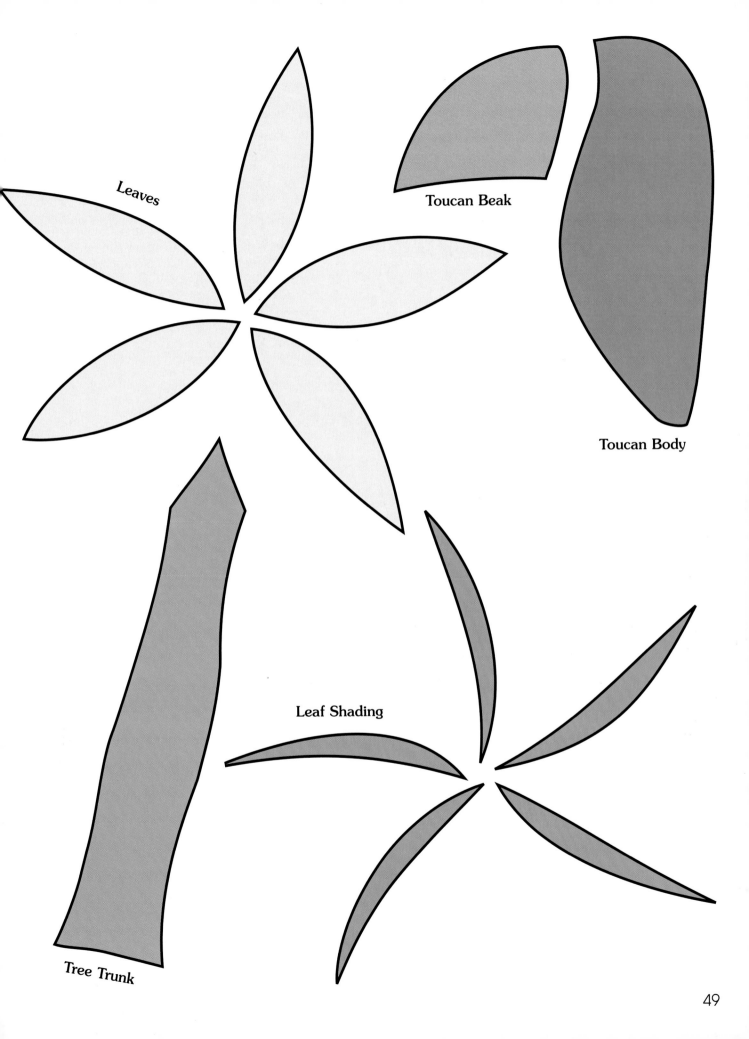

Leaves

Toucan Beak

Toucan Body

Tree Trunk

Leaf Shading

49

SAFARI NIGHTSTAND

(Photo, pg. 45)

SUPPLIES
You will need one folding TV tray and fabrics for cover and topper.

INSTRUCTIONS
1. Fold out tray.
2. For cover, on side of tray facing you, measure from floor to top of tray, across tray, and down to floor on the opposite side; add 1". Measure width of tray on the same side; add one 1". Cut a piece of cover fabric the determined measurements.
3. Turn tray one-quarter turn to an unmeasured side. Repeat Step 2 to cut a second piece of cover fabric. Press all edges of covers 1/4" to wrong side twice. Topstitch to secure.
4. For topper, measure length of tray; add 1". Measure width of tray; add 22". Cut a piece of topper fabric the determined measurements.
5. Mark centers of short ends on topper. Measure and mark 8 1/2" from one short end on both long sides; repeat for remaining end. Using a ruler or yardstick, draw a line from each 8 1/2" mark to nearest center mark. Cut along drawn lines to make points on topper.
6. Press diagonal edges of topper 1/4" to wrong side twice; topstitch to secure. Press remaining edges of topper 1/4" to wrong side twice; topstitch to secure. Place covers and topper on tray.

ZEBRA RUG

(Photo, pg. 44)

SUPPLIES
You will need a piece of upholstery-weight zebra-print fabric cut to desired finished size of rug, fabric for border, jumbo rickrack, and a glue gun.

INSTRUCTIONS
1. For each side of border, cut a 4"w strip of border fabric the length of side plus 1". Press short ends of border strips 1/4" to wrong side twice; topstitch to secure.
2. Press one long edge of each border strip 1/2" to wrong side. Using a 1/2" seam allowance and matching raw edges, sew right side of strips to wrong side of zebra print fabric. Flip strips over to right side. Press strips flat and topstitch close to long pressed edges.
3. Glue rickrack along inside of border.

"MOSQUITO NETTING" WINDOW TREATMENT

(Photo, pg. 44)

SUPPLIES
You will need natural cheesecloth, natural raffia, and two purchased beanbag monkeys.

INSTRUCTIONS
1. Drape desired length of fabric over curtain rod. Use raffia to tie fabric to each end of rod.
2. Hang monkeys on ends of rod.

BAMBOO HEADBOARD

(Photo, pg. 46)

SUPPLIES

You will need a purchased wooden headboard (we used a very simple unfinished headboard), natural muslin for back of headboard (optional), drill, two $1^1/_2$" dia. bamboo poles cut 8" taller than total height of headboard, $1/_2$" dia. bamboo poles cut 4 to 6 inches shorter than total height of headboard, $2^1/_2$" long and 1" long nails, hammer, natural raffia, and glue gun.

Note: Pre-drilling nail holes in bamboo will help prevent splitting.

INSTRUCTIONS

1. For headboard, use $2^1/_2$" nails to nail one $1^1/_2$" dia. pole to each side of headboard. Beginning on one side of headboard, use raffia to tie a $1/_2$" dia. pole to $1^1/_2$" dia. pole; glue smaller pole to headboard. Tie a second small pole to the first and glue second pole to headboard. Continue tying and gluing poles until headboard is covered. Tie last $1/_2$" dia. pole to remaining $1^1/_2$" dia. pole. Use 1" nails to secure every fourth or fifth $1/_2$" pole to headboard.
2. If desired, use 1" nails to tack muslin to back of headboard.

JUNGLE CANOPY

(Photo, pg. 43)

SUPPLIES

You will need natural cheesecloth or other sheer cotton fabric, two curtain rods same width as bed, hardware to mount one curtain rod on wall, and two decorative ceiling hooks.

INSTRUCTIONS

1. Mount one curtain rod to wall above headboard and just below ceiling. Use hooks to hang remaining curtain rod over end of bed parallel to first rod.
2. Measure width and length of bed; multiply each measurement by 2.5. Cut a piece of cheesecloth the determined measurements. Fold cheesecloth in half lengthwise. Leaving an opening for turning, use a $1/_2$" seam allowance to sew edges together. Turn right side out. Sew opening closed; press. Drape cheesecloth over rods and allow to hang behind headboard.

LION PILLOW

(Photo, pg. 46)

SUPPLIES
You will need a purchased square knife-edge pillow, braided fringe, braided raffia, natural raffia, 2"w heart-shaped black button for nose, two 1" and ¹/₂" dia. buttons for eyes, two ¹/₄" dia. buttons for mouth, narrow jute, fabric glue, and a glue gun.

Note: Use fabric glue for all gluing unless otherwise indicated.

INSTRUCTIONS
1. For ears, use natural raffia to gather and tie approx. 4" of two corners of pillow. For mane, glue fringe on front of pillow to make face shape, adding extra pieces at top and bottom for fullness.
2. Sew buttons to pillow for eyes and nose. Glue jute to pillow for mouth. Use glue gun to glue one button to each side of mouth. Cut two 3¹/₂" piece from raffia braid for eyebrows; glue to pillow. For whiskers, tie a knot in centers of two small bundle of raffia; glue knots to pillow.

TASSELED AND TIED PILLOWS

(Photos, pgs. 45 and 46)

SUPPLIES
You will need purchased pillows, 8"w strips of print fabric, natural raffia or raffia tassels, and pony beads or assorted size buttons.

For raffia bundle pillow, you will also need a glue gun.

INSTRUCTIONS
1. **For large tassel pillow,** sew loop of tassel to pillow. Sew buttons over loop.
2. **For beaded raffia pillow,** tie a fabric strip around pillow. Knot raffia around center of fabric strip. Thread beads onto ends of raffia; knot raffia to secure.
3. **For raffia bundle pillow,** wrap and glue center of fabric strip around a handful of raffia. Sew ends of fabric to back of pillow.
4. **For small tassel pillow,** knot a fabric strip around pillow; trim ends. Secure knot with a few stitches if necessary. Sew loop of tassel to fabric at knot. Sew buttons over loop. Sew buttons to pillow.

ZEBRA PILLOW

(Photo, pg. 45)

SUPPLIES
You will need a purchased pillow, 12" square of zebra-print fabric, braided fringe, raffia braid, narrow jute, black shank buttons for eyes, assorted size buttons for nose and corners of pillow, tracing paper, fabric glue, and a glue gun.

Note: Use fabric glue for all gluing unless otherwise indicated.

INSTRUCTIONS
1. Trace zebra pattern, onto tracing paper; cut out. Use pattern to cut one zebra shape from fabric. Use fabric glue to glue shape to center of pillow. Glue jute around zebra shape. Cut a 6" length of fringe. Fold fringe piece in half. Use glue gun to glue fringe piece to zebra for mane.
2. Glue a length of fringe around edges of pillow. Glue braid to top of fringe. Sew eyes to zebra. Sew one large button to zebra for nose. Sew remaining buttons to corners of pillow.

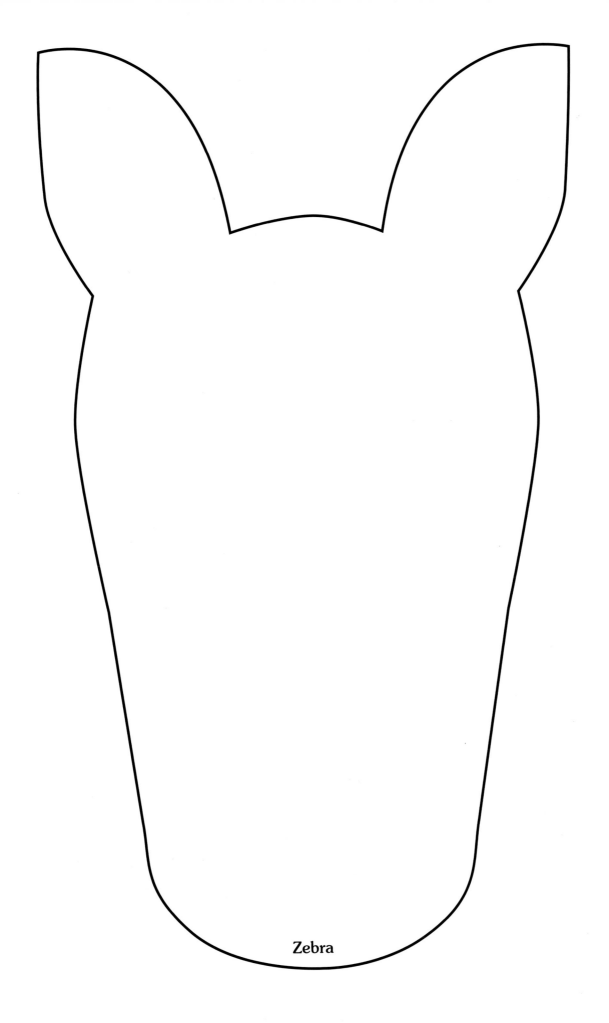

Zebra

the magical GARDEN

Who wouldn't love to live in this **enchanted garden** of fantasy flowers and cuddly **bunnies**? To make your own crafting **magic**, turn to page 60 for project instructions.

$\mathbf{A}$ lovely **Window Box Mirror** reflects sweetness from its place on the darling **Skirted Vanity Table**. Providing extra seating for visitors, the **Padded Chest** is also a handy place to store playthings and other treasures.

Everything grows very well in this magical garden! The **Trellis Headboard** holds vines and flowers that never need watering. And our super-easy **Patchwork Duvet** and whimsical array of pillows are absolutely charming. There's even a floral **Skirted Stool** so a special young lady can sit and visit with our truly enchanting **Garden Rabbit**. To make the cute character, simply add ears, a face, and clothing to a purchased soft doll body!

TRELLIS HEADBOARD

(Photo, pg. 59)

SUPPLIES

You will need twin-size wooden headboard, batting and fabric to cover headboard, staple gun, glue gun, silk greenery vine, silk flowers, 1½"w ribbon, 13"h wire garden edging, wire cutters, and hardware and tools to attach headboard to bed frame.

INSTRUCTIONS

1. To cover headboard, measure width and height of headboard. Cut a piece of batting and fabric 10" larger than determined measurements. Center batting on front of headboard. Staple edges of batting to back of headboard, smoothing batting across front. Repeat to staple fabric to headboard.
2. Cut garden edging in pieces to fit around headboard. With 6½" of edging extending beyond edges of headboard, glue edging pieces to back of headboard.
3. Glue silk vine to top and side edges on front of headboard. Arrange and glue flowers and ribbon to vine and headboard.
4. Attach headboard to bed frame.

PATCHWORK DUVET

(Photo, pg. 59)

SUPPLIES

You will need assorted fabrics for top, twin-size flat sheet (at least 69" x 94") for back, and 64" of 1"w hook and loop fastener.

Note: Finished duvet holds a 66" x 86" comforter. Use a ¼" seam allowance for all sewing and sew with right sides together unless otherwise indicated.

INSTRUCTIONS

1. Cut a 4¼" x 68½" strip of fabric for top hem facing; set aside. Cut eighty-eight 9" squares from assorted fabrics.
2. Sew eight squares together to make a 68½" long strip. Repeat to make a total of eleven strips. Sew long edges of strips together to make front; press.
3. Press one long edge of top hem facing ¼" to wrong side twice; topstitch to secure. Sew remaining long edge of hem facing to one short edge of front. Press seam toward hem facing. Topstitch along seam allowance. Press hem facing to right side of front; stitch along short ends to secure.
4. Center front on back with top edges even. Trim any excess fabric from back. Sew front to back along side and bottom edges. Turn right side out. Follow manufacturer's instructions to sew hook and loop fastener inside top edges of duvet.

DUST RUFFLE

(Photo, pg. 55)

SUPPLIES

You will need fabric for ruffle, 1"w gathering tape, and large safety pins.

Note: Dust ruffle is three finished pieces.

INSTRUCTIONS

1. To determine height of all dust ruffle pieces, measure from floor to top of box springs; add 2". For length of foot piece, measure width of box springs at foot; multiply by 2.5. For length of each side piece, measure side of box springs; multiply by 2.5. Piecing fabric as necessary, cut one foot piece and two side pieces.
2. Press short edges of each piece ¼" to wrong side twice; topstitch to secure. For hem, press one long edge of each piece ¼" to wrong side twice; topstitch to secure. For top edge of each piece, press remaining long edges ½" then 1" to wrong side; topstitch to secure.
3. Follow manufacturer's instructions to sew gathering tape along wrong side of top edge of each dust ruffle piece. Pull strings, gathering ruffles to fit box springs; knot or tie strings to secure. Use safety pins to pin gathered edges of dust ruffles to top of box springs.

PADDED CHEST

(Photo, pg. 56)

SUPPLIES

You will need a wooden toy box with removable seat; primer; antique white latex paint; non-toxic brush-on sealer; dark yellow, light pink, pink, blue, light green, and green acrylic paint; tracing paper; transfer paper; black permanent fine-point marker; fabric to cover seat; and a staple gun.

INSTRUCTIONS

1. Remove seat from toy box. Read **Preparing to Paint**, **Painting**, **Transferring Patterns**, and **Painting Details**, pgs. 110 and 111.

2. Prepare box for painting. Paint box antique white. Paint edge of lid with light pink and pink stripes. Paint bottom edge of box blue. Paint details on bottom edge dark yellow.
3. Transfer flower patterns, pg. 63, to front and sides of toy chest. Paint designs according to patterns. Use marker to outline designs.
4. Apply sealer to toy box.
5. To cover seat, measure width and length of seat. Cut a piece of fabric 8" larger than determined measurements. Staple edges of fabric to back of seat, smoothing fabric over front. Reattach seat to toy chest.

PILLOW SHAM

(Photo, pg. 59)

SUPPLIES

You will need a 21½" x 28" piece of print fabric for front, two 16" x 21½" pieces of fabric for back, and a ¼ yd piece of fabric for ruffle.

Note: Sham fits a standard-size pillow. Use a ½" seam allowance for all sewing unless otherwise indicated.

INSTRUCTIONS

1. Press one long edge of each back piece ½" to wrong side twice; topstitch to secure.

2. For ruffle, cut six 7" x 42" strips from fabric. Sew short ends of strips together and trim to 6¾ yds. Press one short end ½" to wrong side. Matching wrong sides, press strip in half lengthwise. Baste ¼" from long raw edges.
3. Matching raw edges, pull basting threads, gathering strip to fit around all edges of front with ends overlapping 1". Baste ruffle to right side of front, leaving 2" of ruffle ends free. Remove gathering thread from approx. 2" of pressed end. Insert raw end into pressed end. Baste gathered edges of ends to front. Hand sew opening in ruffle closed.
4. Matching right sides and raw edges, place backs on front with finished edges of backs overlapping at center. Sew backs to front along edges of front. Clip corners and turn sham right side out.

POM-POM CIRCLE PILLOW

(Photo, pg. 59)

SUPPLIES

You will need two 20" squares of chenille fabric, 1⅔ yds of pom-pom fringe, polyester fiberfill, 1" dia. button, 1½" dia. covered button kit, print fabric to cover button, 3" dia. or larger silk flower, wire cutters, thumbtack, string, and a fabric marking pen.

INSTRUCTIONS

1. Read **Cutting a Fabric Circle**, pg. 111, and use a 9" measurement for string to cut two 18" dia. circles from fabric squares.

2. Matching edges and trimming ends to fit, baste fringe along edge of one circle. Matching right sides, leaving an opening for turning, and using a ½" seam allowance, sew front to back.
3. Clip curves and turn pillow right side out. Stuff pillow with fiberfill. Hand sew opening closed.
4. Follow manufacturer's instructions to cover 1½" button with fabric. Cut flower from stem. With button centered in flower and 1" dia. button on back of pillow for support, stitch through pillow to sew covered button and flower to center front of pillow.

PAINTED GARDEN PILLOW

(Photo, pg. 59)

SUPPLIES

You will need two 11" x 13" pieces of fabric for front and back; 1/2 yd of 45"w fabric for ruffle; dark yellow, light pink, pink, blue, light green, and green acrylic paint; tracing paper; transfer paper; plastic wrap; 12" x 14" or larger piece of cardboard; T-pins; black permanent fine-point marker, and polyester fiberfill.

Note: Use a 1/2" seam allowance for all sewing unless otherwise indicated.

INSTRUCTIONS

1. Read **Transferring Patterns**, pg. 111. Trace flower patterns, pg. 63, onto tracing paper. Transfer patterns to center of front.

2. Wrap cardboard with plastic wrap. Pin front to cardboard. Paint designs according to patterns; allow to dry. Outline designs with black marker.

3. For ruffle, cut three 6" x 42" strips from fabric. Sew short ends of strips together and trim to 3 1/3 yds. Press one short end 1/2" to wrong side. Matching wrong sides, press strip in half lengthwise. Baste 1/4" from long raw edges.

4. Matching raw edges, pull basting threads, gathering strip to fit around all edges of front with ends overlapping 1". Baste ruffle to right side of front, leaving 2" of ruffle ends free. Remove gathering thread from approx. 2" of pressed end. Insert raw end into pressed end. Baste gathered edges of ends to front. Hand sew opening in ruffle closed.

5. Matching right sides and raw edges and leaving an opening for turning, sew front to back, curving seams at corners. Clip corners and turn pillow right side out. Stuff pillow with fiberfill. Hand sew opening closed.

POTTED FANTASY FLOWERS

(Photo, pg. 58)

SUPPLIES

You will need three 4 1/2" dia. clay flowerpots; 36" length of 1/16" dia. dowel; peach, pink, dark pink, and green acrylic paint; non-toxic spray sealer; paper-backed fusible web; poster board; craft knife; assorted pink and green fabrics for flowers; tan fabric; tracing paper; yellow and pink 1/8" dia. satin rattail cording; one 14" length each of yellow, pink, and green 1/16"w satin ribbon; floral foam; and a glue gun.

INSTRUCTIONS

1. Paint dowel green. Paint flowerpots as desired. Paint stripes on rims. Apply sealer to flowerpots and dowel.

2. Apply fusible web to wrong side of fabrics; do not remove paper backing. Separately trace each piece of blossoms, blossom centers, and leaves from flower patterns, pg. 63, onto tracing paper; cut out. Reverse patterns. Draw around patterns on web side of fabrics; cut out.

3. Fuse blossoms and leaves to poster board. Fuse blossom centers to blossoms; cut out blossoms and leaves. For details, glue pieces of cording to leaves and blossom centers. Cut dowel into three unequal lengths. Glue leaves and blossoms to dowels. Tie one ribbon into a bow around each dowel.

4. Glue floral foam inside pots. Cut a 6" square of tan fabric for each pot. Cover foam with fabric pieces. Use craft knife to cut a hole in center of fabric. Insert one flower into each pot.

WINDOW BOX MIRROR

(Photo, pg. 56)

SUPPLIES

You will need a wooden window box with mirror, antique white latex paint, non-toxic spray sealer, silk greenery and flowers, wire cutters, floral foam, and glue gun.

INSTRUCTIONS

1. Remove mirror from window box. Read **Preparing to Paint** and **Painting**, pg. 110, to paint window box. Apply sealer to window box. Replace mirror.

2. Glue floral foam in box. Arrange some of the greenery and flowers in foam. Cut remaining flowers from stem. Glue greenery and flowers along top of window.

Flowers

SKIRTED STOOL

(Photo, pg. 57)

SUPPLIES

You will need a $16^1/2$" dia. x 18"h decorator stool kit, craft drill, staple gun, glue gun, long needle, 2" thick foam, 2 yds of 2"w gathered lace, one 36" square each of batting and fabric for seat, $1^1/4$ yds of 45"w fabric for ruffle, 2 yds of 45"w fabric for skirt, heavy-duty thread, large silk flower, wire cutters, $1^1/2$" dia. covered button kit, and a fabric scrap to cover button.

Note: Use a $1/2$" seam allowance for all sewing unless otherwise indicated.

INSTRUCTIONS

1. Drill two small holes 1" apart through center of stool seat.
2. Cut foam same size as stool seat; glue to seat 1" from edges. With foam on top of stool seat, cover seat with batting and seat fabric; smooth to bottom of seat. Staple batting and fabric to bottom of seat.
3. Follow manufacturer's instructions to cover button with fabric. Cut flower from stem. Thread needle with 2 to 3 lengths of heavy-duty thread. With button centered in flower and passing needle through holes in seat, stitch button and flower to seat. Knot thread ends at bottom of seat to secure.
4. Cut two 21" x 72" pieces from fabric for skirt. Sew short ends together to make a tube. For hem, press one raw edge $3/4$" to wrong side twice; topstitch to secure.
5. Cut five 8" x 45" strips from fabric for ruffle. Sew short ends together to make a tube. Matching wrong sides and raw edges, press tube in half. Baste $1/4$" from raw edges. Place tube for ruffle over tube for skirt. Gather ruffle to fit skirt. Matching raw edges, sew ruffle to skirt.
6. To gather skirt, baste around skirt $1/2$" from top edge. Pull thread ends to gather skirt to fit seat. With top edge of lace $1/4$" from top edge of ruffle, sew lace to ruffle and skirt. Concealing seams under seat, staple top of skirt to bottom of seat.
7. Follow manufacturer's instructions to assemble stool.

SKIRTED VANITY TABLE

(Photo, pg. 57)

SUPPLIES

You will need a 20"d x 42"w x 30"h decorator vanity table kit, 3 yds of 45"w print fabric, 2 yds of 45"w border fabric, 3 yds of pom-pom fringe, $1^1/2$ yd of $7/8$"w wired ribbon, $2/3$ yd of (at least) 45"w fabric for tabletop, 2 yds of 45"w lining fabric, 6 yds of $1^1/4$"w shirring tape, 7" dia. salad plate, fabric marking pen, glue gun, #10 carpet tacks, craft drill (optional), and spray adhesive.

Note: Match right sides and use a $1/2$" seam allowance unless otherwise indicated. If using a particle board table, drill pilot holes in center of tabletop edge before nailing to avoid cracks or breaks in tabletop.

INSTRUCTIONS

1. Spray top and sides of tabletop with adhesive. Spread fabric over tabletop with right side up; cut fabric even with bottom edge of tabletop.
2. For table skirt, cut two 21" x 3 yd strips from print fabric. Sew short ends together to make a 6 yd strip. Cut three 9" x 2 yd strips from border fabric and lining fabric. Sew short ends of border strip together and short ends of lining together to make two 6 yd strips.
3. For scallops, draw a line $1/2$" from one long edge on wrong side of lining. Draw a second line $2^3/4$" from first line. Align edge of plate with first drawn line and short edge of lining. Draw around plate on lining between drawn lines. Continue drawing scallops along lining. Press top (unmarked edge) of lining $1/2$" to wrong side.
4. For skirt, matching long edges, sew border to print fabric piece; press seam allowance toward border.
5. Matching long edges, sew along scallop lines to sew border and lining pieces together. Cut away excess fabric below scallops, leaving a $1/4$" seam allowance. Sew along short ends. Clip curves and corners. Turn border right side out; press. Topstitch to secure lining to seam allowance.
6. Press top edge of skirt $5/8$" to wrong side. Follow manufacturer's instructions to sew shirring tape to wrong side of skirt along top edge.
7. Follow manufacturer's instructions to assemble table.
8. With top edge of skirt even with top edge of table, tack skirt to center front of table. Nail skirt ends to back of tabletop. Pull gathering strings to gather fabric to table. Tack skirt to table at 3" intervals. Glue gathers between tacks to secure. Beginning and ending at back of table and trimming fringe to fit, glue fringe to table over tacks.
9. Cut a 12" length of ribbon. Pull wire on one side of ribbon to shape ribbon into a doubled circle. Tie one yard of ribbon into a bow. Cut a pom-pom ball from excess fringe. Glue ball to circle. Glue circle to bow. Glue bow to center front of skirt.

GARDEN RABBIT

(Photo, pg. 58)

SUPPLIES

You will need a 22"h blank muslin doll form, 1/3 yd of ecru chenille fabric, pink and brown embroidery floss, paper-backed fusible web, two 1/2" dia. white buttons, fabric scraps for appliqués, two 3/4" pieces of 1/2"w adhesive hook and loop fastener strip, 1 yd of 45"w checked fabric, 1/2 yd of striped fabric, seam ripper, artificial flowers, wire cutters, glue gun, one yd of 1/8"w satin ribbon, tracing paper, and cosmetic blush.

Note: Match right sides and use a 1/4" seam allowance unless otherwise indicated.

INSTRUCTIONS

1. Trace rabbit face pattern onto a 4" square of tracing paper. Center face pattern on doll's head; pin in place. Read **Embroidery Stitches**, pg. 111. Work Backstitches and Satin Stitches to embroider face on doll's head. Carefully tear away tracing paper.

2. Trace ear pattern onto tracing paper; cut out. Using pattern, cut four ears from chenille fabric. Leaving straight edge open for turning, sew two ear pieces together. Repeat for second ear. Clip point and turn right side out. Fold ear in half lengthwise at straight edge. Sew across ear just above straight edge to secure. Sew ears to head.

3. Cut flowers from stems. Glue flowers to head between ears. Apply cosmetic blush to rabbit's face.

4. Matching arrows and dotted lines, trace top and bottom of pants pattern, pg. 66, onto tracing paper. Cut four pants pieces from striped fabric.

5. Read **Tracing Patterns**, pg. 111. Trace jacket patterns onto tracing paper. Fold checked fabric in half. Cutting through both layers of fabric, cut four front pieces and two back pieces from checked fabric. For sleeves, cut two 5" x 10" pieces each from checked fabric and striped fabric. For pockets, cut two 3" x 5" pieces from checked fabric.

6. For pants front, match edges and sew curved (seat) edges of two pants pieces together; press. Repeat to make pants back. Sew front and back together along inseams and side seams. Press waist and bottom of legs 1/4", then 1/2" to wrong side; topstitch to secure. Turn pants right side out; press.

7. Use seam ripper to open two 3/8" holes 1/2" apart in center front of waistband. Thread ribbon through waist of pants. Place pants on rabbit and tie ribbon ends to secure. Knot ribbon ends.

8. For jacket, sew two jacket fronts to one jacket back along shoulders and side seams; press. Repeat to make jacket lining. Sew jacket and lining together along neck, front, and waist edges. Turn right side out; press.

9. Sew short edges of each sleeve piece together, forming four tubes. Turn checked tubes right side out. Aligning seams, place one striped tube over each checked tube. Sew tubes together along one long edge to form sleeves. Turn right side out; press. Matching checked side of sleeve and front of jacket and with sleeve seams at underarms, sew sleeves to armholes; press. Fold sleeves up 1 1/2".

10. Press short edges, then long edges of pockets 1/4" to wrong side. Pin pockets to jacket front 1 1/4" from bottom and 1 7/8" from front edge. Topstitch sides and bottom of pocket.

11. For appliqués, fuse web to wrong side of fabric scraps. Cut a 3/8" x 5" piece of fabric for stem. Trace appliqué patterns separately onto tracing paper; do not remove paper backing. Reverse blossom patterns. Draw around blossom and blossom center twice and leaf five times on web side of fabrics; cut out. With stem end at bottom on one pocket, fuse appliqué pieces to front of jacket. Clip stem in two above pocket; press.

12. Use pink floss to sew two buttons to one side of jacket front. Place jacket on rabbit. Adhere hook and loop fasteners to jacket under buttons.

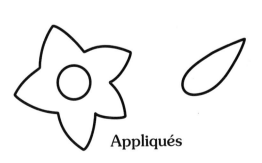

Appliqués

Ear

Rabbit Face

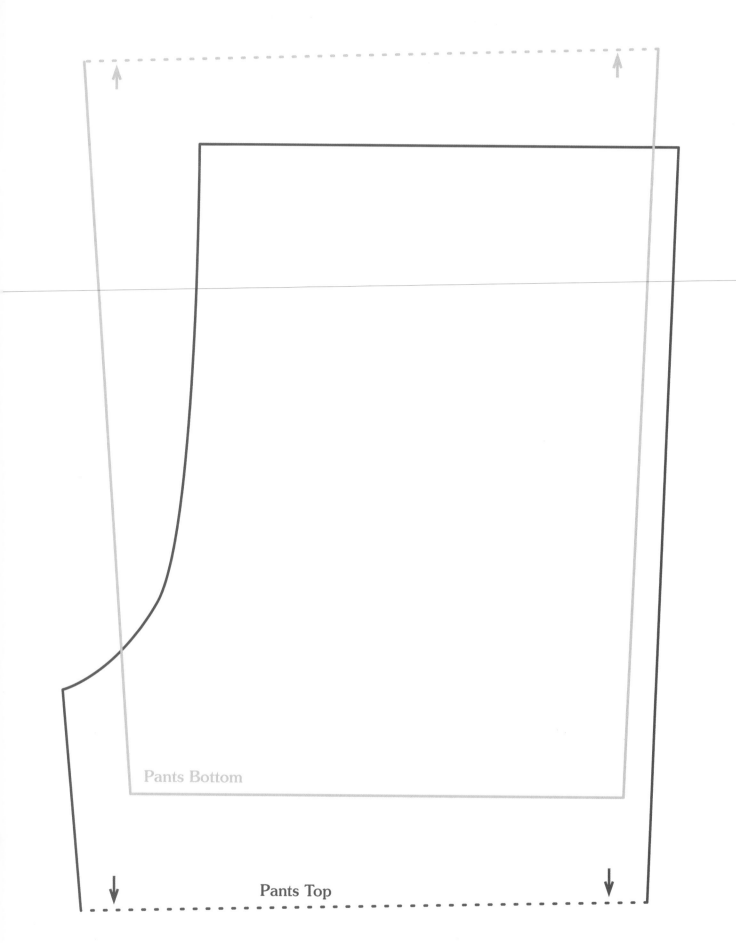

Pants Bottom

Pants Top

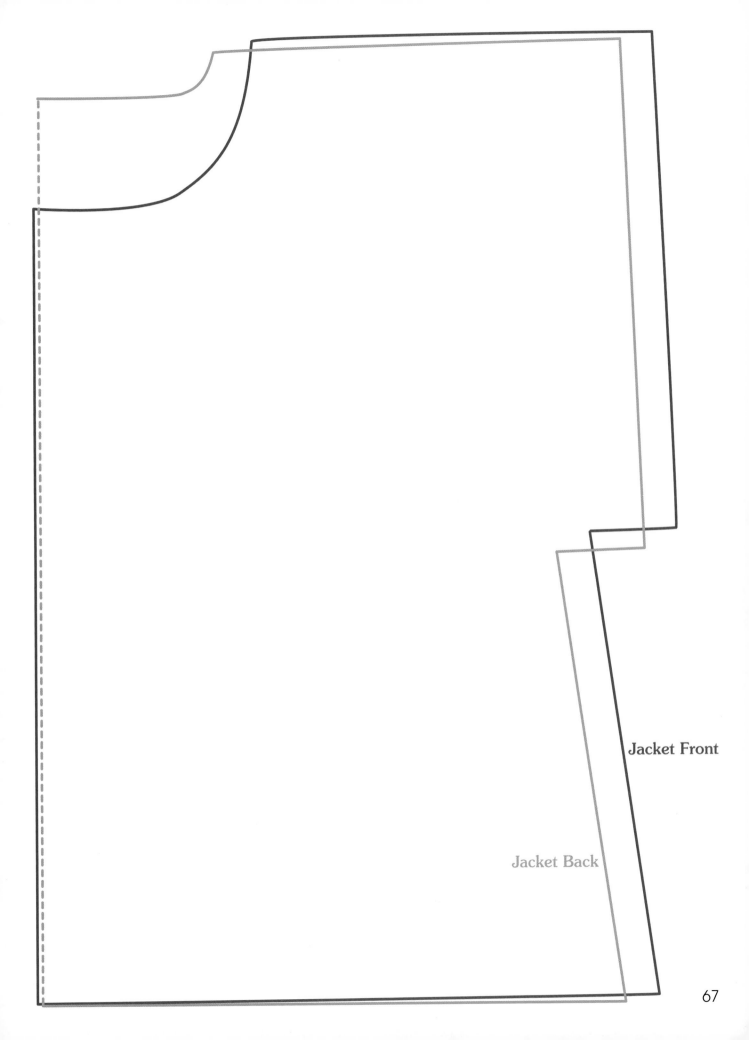

Jacket Front

Jacket Back

67

AHOY, MATE!

There's smooth **sailing** ahead for the captain of these **seaworthy** quarters! Ready-made bedspreads help the bunks stay shipshape, while a clever **Lighthouse Lamp** keeps little feet **on course** at night. Cast off to create these coastal delights, beginning on page 74.

Display photos of the whole crew in these **"Memory Preserver" Photo Frames**, then relax in the fun **Sea Breezes Chair**. Or lounge in the roomy window seat, made comfy by a whole fleet of easily crafted pillows. To make the window seat cushion, just fold a sturdy rib-cord bedspread around a thick foam piece and secure with a few stitches. Any leftover bedspread fabric makes a great backdrop for the bright **Signal Flag Valance**.

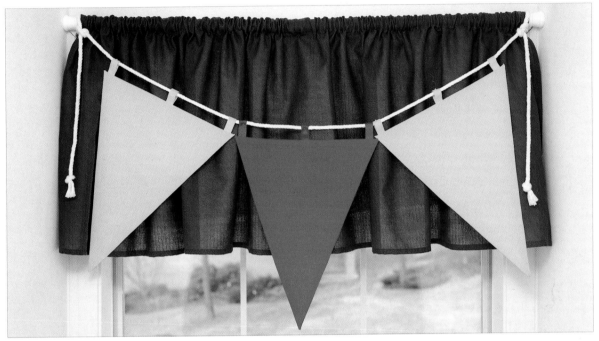

Our curious **Seagull** perches on one of the **Boardwalk Headboards** to check out a fisherman's catch of sea shells and snappy **Lobsters**. Would you ever guess the recycled **Lighthouse Nightstand** gets its easy good looks from a cardboard-backed print? And although it looks like a sailor's duffel bag, the **Bed Bolster** is actually a roll of batting wrapped in a nautical print. Toss in the personalized **Life Preserver Pillow** and this room sets sail for oceans of fun!

LIGHTHOUSE NIGHTSTAND

(Photo, pg. 72)

SUPPLIES

You will need a nightstand with removable panel in door; four 4½"w papier-mâché stars; primer; white latex paint; light blue, blue, dark blue, and brown acrylic paint; non-toxic brush-on sealer, 6" silver flag cleat; cardboard; lighthouse print; staple gun; and a glue gun.

INSTRUCTIONS

1. Remove door pull from door. Remove panel from door; set aside. Read **Preparing to Paint** and **Painting**, pg. 110. Paint nightstand and stars white. For a weathered look, drybrush acrylic paints over nightstand and stars. Apply sealer to nightstand and stars.
2. Draw around removed panel on print and cardboard; cut out print and cardboard just inside drawn line. Place print and cardboard in door; staple to secure.
3. Install cleat for door handle. Glue stars to door.

BOARDWALK HEADBOARDS

(Photo, pg. 73)

SUPPLIES

You will need a 4 ft x 8½ ft wooden fence section (makes two twin-size headboards); two twin-size bed frames; primer; white and blue latex paint; non-toxic brush-on sealer; fishnet; saw; hardware and craft drill to attach headboards to bed frames; glue gun; **Lobster** (pg. 78); and seashells.

Note: Use craft glue for all gluing unless otherwise indicated.

INSTRUCTIONS

1. Before cutting fence, make sure the bolt holes in headboard end of bed frame will line up with fence pickets or rails. Cut fence section into two 38" long sections, (you will have one or more scrap pieces). Mark and drill holes in fence sections to align with bolt holes in bed frames.
2. Read **Preparing to Paint** and **Painting**, pg. 110, to paint headboards blue. For a weathered look, drybrush white paint over blue. Apply sealer to headboards.
5. Arrange fishnet on headboards. Use glue gun to glue lobster and seashells to each fishnet. Attach headboards to bed frames.

SEAGULL

Photo, pg. 72)

SUPPLIES

You will need foam core board; craft glue; glue gun; tracing paper; white, blue, and yellow acrylic paint; wooden skewer; straight pin with round black head; craft knife; and a cutting mat.

1. For seagull body, glue five 9" squares of foam core board together in a stack; weight with a heavy book until dry. Trace seagull patterns separately onto tracing paper; cut out. Draw around body pattern on stacked foam core board; cut out. Draw around wing patterns on a single layer of foam core board; cut out.

2. To give seagull pieces a carved look, use craft knife to shave edges of pieces. Paint body white. Paint wing pieces blue, then drybrush white. Paint skewer yellow. Use craft glue to glue wing and body pieces together. For eye, insert pin into seagull. For beak and leg, cut one 2" piece and one 6" piece from skewer. Insert skewer pieces into seagull; glue to secure. Glue seagull to chair back or headboard.

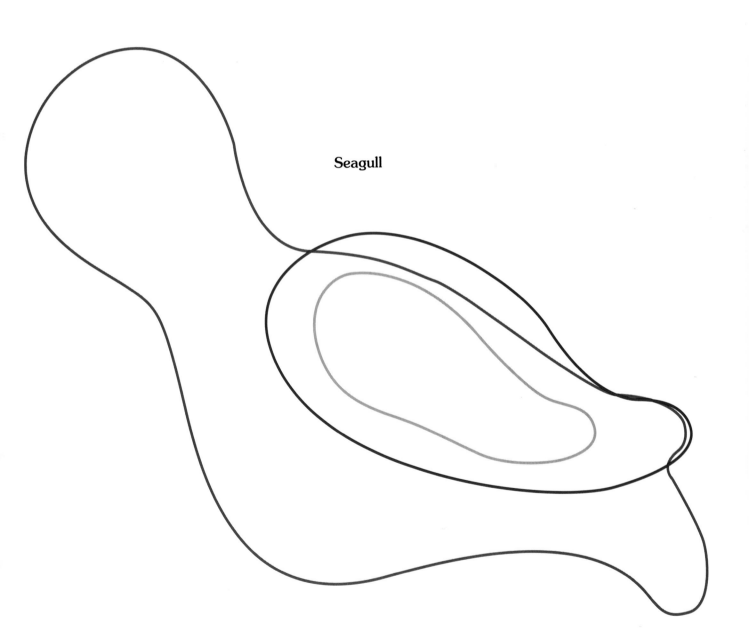

Seagull

75

PADDLE PEG RACK

(Photo, pg. 70)

SUPPLIES

You will need a wooden paddle-shaped peg rack, floor wax, wood-tone spray, white acrylic paint, non-toxic spray sealer, sandpaper, and sawtooth hanger kit.

INSTRUCTIONS

1. Read **Preparing to Paint** and **Painting**, pg. 110. Apply wood-tone spray to peg rack.
2. Apply floor wax in random areas over peg rack. Paint peg rack white. Lightly sand peg rack, removing paint over waxed areas. Apply sealer to peg rack.
3. Mount sawtooth hangers on back of peg rack.

SEA BREEZES CHAIR

(Photo, pg. 70)

SUPPLIES

You will need a wooden Adirondack chair; primer; light blue latex paint; tracing paper; transfer paper; white, yellow, red, blue, and black acrylic paint; non-toxic brush-on sealer; two $4^1/_2$"w papier-mâché stars; glue gun; 4" thick foam for cushion; fabric for cover; and $^3/_8$" dia. cord.

Note: Match right sides and use a $^1/_2$" seam allowance for all sewing unless otherwise indicated.

INSTRUCTIONS

1. Read **Preparing to Paint** and **Painting**, pg. 110. Paint chair with light blue latex paint. Paint stars white. For a weathered look, drybrush blue acrylic paint over stars.
2. If desired, read **Sizing Patterns**, pg. 110, to enlarge or reduce sailboat pattern (sailboat on our chair measures $12^1/_4$"w x $14^3/_8$"h). Read **Transferring Patterns**, pg. 111. Transfer sailboat pattern to back of chair. Use acrylic paint to paint sailboat design.
3. Glue stars to chair arms. Apply sealer to chair.
4. For chair cushion, measure seat of chair from front to back and side to side. Cut a piece of foam the determined measurements. For top and bottom of cover, cut two pieces of fabric 1" larger than determined measurements.
5. For side of cover, measure around sides of foam piece; add 3". Cut a 5"w piece of fabric the determined measurement.
6. Press one short end of side piece 1" to wrong side. Beginning at pressed end, sew side piece to all edges of top piece; clip corners. Sew ends of side together. Leaving back edge open for insertion of foam, sew side piece to bottom piece; turn right side out. Insert cushion into cover. Leaving a 2" long opening at center of seam, hand sew opening closed. On the same (back) side, make a 2" long opening in remaining seam. Inserting cord ends into openings, sew cord around top and bottom of cushion. Hand sew openings closed.

Sailboat

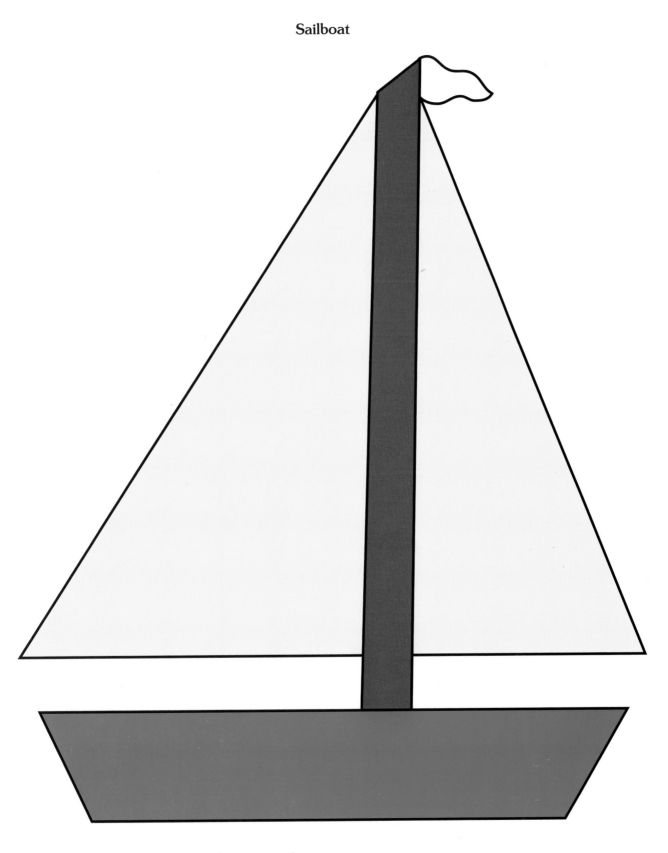

Leisure Arts, Inc., grants permission to the owner of this book to photocopy the design on this page for personal use only.

LIFE PRESERVER PILLOW

(Photo, pg. 73)

SUPPLIES

You will need two 22" squares of white fabric, fabric marking pen, string, thumbtack, four 14" lengths of 1"w red grosgrain ribbon, 2 yds of $^3/_8$" dia. cord, $1^1/_2$"h fusible letters, polyester fiberfill, and a glue gun.

INSTRUCTIONS

1. Stack fabric squares with edges even. Read **Cutting a Fabric Circle**, pg. 111. Use a $3^1/_2$" measurement to cut a 7" dia. inner circle and a 10" measurement to cut a 20" dia. outer circle from fabric for pillow front and back.
2. Centering between edges to keep letters even, follow manufacturer's instructions to fuse letters to right side of pillow front.
3. Matching right sides, leaving an opening for turning, and using a $^1/_2$" seam allowance, sew front and back together. Clip seam allowances and turn pillow right side out. Stuff pillow with fiberfill. Sew opening closed.
4. On each length of ribbon, fold one end 1" to wrong side to form a loop; glue to secure. Wrap and glue ribbon lengths around pillow, placing raw ends under loops on outer edge of pillow. Thread cord through loops; tie cord ends together at bottom of pillow.

LOBSTER

(Photo, pg. 72)

SUPPLIES

You will need an 8" x 10" foam food tray, red and black acrylic paint, foam brushes, non-toxic spray sealer, two 4mm black beads, two 8" lengths of 18-gauge florist wire, tracing paper, craft knife, cutting mat, craft glue, and glue gun.

INSTRUCTIONS

1. Read **Tracing Patterns**, pg. 111. Trace lobster pattern onto tracing paper; cut out.
2. Place pattern in food tray with tail on upturned edge. Use a dull pencil to draw around pattern on tray; draw over detail lines to indent lines into tray. Use craft knife to cut out lobster.
3. Apply two coats of red paint to lobster; allow to dry. Apply sealer to lobster.
4. Use craft glue to glue beads to lobster for eyes.
5. For antennae, bend a curve into one end of each wire. Paint wires black. Use glue gun to glue 1" of straight ends to back of lobster.

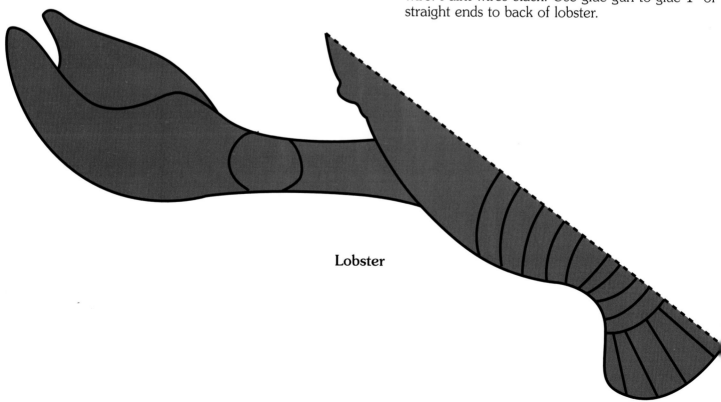

Lobster

SQUARE THROW PILLOWS

(Photo, pg. 71)

SUPPLIES

You will need a 14" square knife-edge pillow form, 30" square of fabric, 4¹/₂"w papier-mâché star, white and blue acrylic paint, non-toxic spray sealer, and a glue gun.

INSTRUCTIONS

1. Read **Painting**, pg. 110. Paint star white. Drybrush star blue. Apply sealer to star.
2. Place fabric wrong side up. Fold right edge of fabric 1" to wrong side. Center pillow form on wrong side of fabric. Bring left then right sides of fabric over pillow form. Hand sew fabric layers together along fold.
3. Fold fabric at ends of pillow, making points in remaining fabric ends. Bring points together over seam. Fold under excess fabric of points, if necessary; sew to center of pillow.
4. Glue star to center of pillow.

SIGNAL FLAG VALANCE

(Photo, pg. 71)

SUPPLIES

You will need a tension rod to fit window, twin-sized ribbed cord bedspread, ³/₈" dia. cord, yellow and red fabrics for pennants, ⁵/₈"w yellow and red grosgrain ribbon, fusible interfacing, ¹/₂"w paper-backed fusible web tape, glue gun, and newspaper or tissue paper.

INSTRUCTIONS

1. For valance, cut bottom 24" from bedspread. If your window is more than 40"w, cut top 24" from bedspread as well. For rod pocket, press raw edge(s) under ¹/₂". Press under 2" again and topstitch to secure. Insert rod in pocket.
2. For pennant pattern, refer to **Fig. 1** to draw a diagonal line across one corner of newspaper at 6" and 15" from corner. Cut out pattern along drawn line.
3. Fold interfacing. Placing 15" edge of pattern on fold, cut three pennants from interfacing. Unfold pennants. Fusing to wrong side of fabrics, fuse one pennant to red fabric and two pennants to yellow fabric. Cut out pennants ¹/₂" from edges of interfacing. Fuse web tape to wrong sides of pennants along all edges. Remove paper backing and fuse all edges ¹/₂" to wrong side.
4. For each pennant, cut three 5" lengths of ribbon in color to match pennant. Fold ribbons in half to form hanging loops. Glue loops to backs of short edges of pennants.
5. Thread cord through hanging loops. Tie one end of cord on each end of rod.

Fig. 1

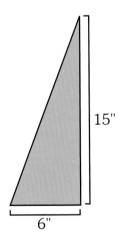

15"

6"

"MEMORY PRESERVER" PHOTO FRAMES

(Photo, pg. 70)

SUPPLIES

For each frame, you will need two 8" squares of white fabric, polyester fiberfill, four 6" lengths of $^1/_4$"w blue grosgrain ribbon, one 25" length and one 14" length of $^1/_8$" dia. white cord, tracing paper, fabric marking pencil, drawing compass, glue gun, poster board, spray mount, color photocopy of photo, and a 2" piece of $^1/_2$" wide self-adhesive hook and loop fastener.

INSTRUCTIONS

1. For pattern, use compass to draw a $6^1/_2$" dia. circle on tracing paper; draw a $2^1/_2$" dia. circle in center of first circle. Cut out along drawn lines.
2. Center pattern on wrong side of one fabric square; use fabric marking pencil to draw around pattern. Do not cut out shape.
3. Place fabric squares right sides together. Leaving an opening in outer circle for turning, sew directly on pencil lines to sew fabric squares together.
4. Adding $^1/_4$" seam allowances, cut out shape; clip seam allowances. Turn shape right side out. Stuff shape with fiberfill. Hand sew opening closed.
5. Overlapping ribbon ends $^1/_2$", glue ribbon ends to inside of frame. On outside seam, pinch ribbon snug to the frame, forming a loop. Glue base of loop to pillow; repeat for remaining ribbons. Thread long cord through loops. Tie cord ends together at bottom of pillow; knot cord ends.
6. Use compass to draw a 4" circle on photocopy and poster board; cut out. Use spray mount to adhere photocopy to poster board. Cut hook and loop fastener into four $^1/_2$" pieces. Adhere fastener pieces to back of frame and front edges of photocopy. Attach photocopy to frame.
7. For hanger, knot ends of remaining cord. Glue ends of hanger to back of frame.

BED BOLSTER

(Photo, pg. 73)

SUPPLIES

You will need $1^1/_4$ yds of 60"w print fabric, batting, and two 18" lengths of $^3/_8$" dia. cord.

INSTRUCTIONS

1. Roll batting into a 13" dia. x 38" long cylinder.
2. Press one long edge of fabric 2" to wrong side. Center length of cylinder on wrong side of remaining long edge of fabric. Roll cylinder in fabric to opposite edge, covering batting in fabric. Hand sew pressed edge of fabric to secure.
3. Knot ends of cord lengths. Gather fabric at ends of bolster; tie gathers with cord. Tuck fabric ends into gathers.

SMALL BOLSTERS

(Photo, pg. 71)

SUPPLIES

For each small bolster, you will need one 24" x 36" piece of fabric, batting, and two 12" lengths of $^3/_8$" dia. cord.

INSTRUCTIONS

1. Roll batting into a 6" dia. x 15" long cylinder.
2. Follow Steps 2 and 3 of Bed Bolster to make bolster.

LIGHTHOUSE LAMP

(Photo, pg. 68)

SUPPLIES

You will need a 5" dia. x 5³/₄"h cardboard container with lid and a 5" dia. x 8¹/₄"h cardboard container (we used powdered drink mix cans); 3" dia. x 3"h can (we used a sweetened condensed milk can); ³/₄" x 7" x 7" box lid for base; 28" of 2¹/₄"h miniature picket fence; hammer; awl; household cement; 8" square of foam core board; drawing compass; craft knife; cutting mat; four toothpicks; craft saw; 2¹/₂"h flat wooden clothespins; white spray primer; masking tape; white, red, and black acrylic paint; non-toxic spray sealer; wood-tone spray; craft drill; glue gun; two 22" lengths of kite string; needle for kite string; hacksaw; ³/₈" dia. threaded I.P. pipe stem; 40" length of floral wire; lamp kit; and a red lampshade.

Note: Use household cement for all gluing unless otherwise indicated.

1. For catwalk, draw around 5³/₄"h container on foam core board. Use compass to draw a second circle 1" outside first circle. Use a craft knife to cut out catwalk along drawn lines.
2. Use hammer and awl to punch a ³/₈" dia. hole in center of closed end of 5³/₄"h container and in center of closed end of can.
3. For lighthouse, glue open ends of 5³/₄"h and 8¹/₄"h containers together. For beacon, aligning holes, glue open end of can to closed end of 5³/₄"h container.
4. For rail posts, use saw to cut "legs" from clothespins; discard "legs."
5. Read **Preparing to Paint** and **Painting**, pg. 110. Apply primer to lighthouse, beacon, catwalk, rail posts, fence, and base.
6. Use masking tape to mask off three evenly spaced 1⁷/₈"w stripes around lighthouse. Paint lighthouse red. Remove tape. Mask painted areas. Paint lighthouse and beacon white. Remove masking tape. Paint a 2" x 3¹/₈" black door on front of lighthouse. Spacing evenly around beacon, use masking tape to mask off ⁷/₈" x 1⁷/₈" "windows." Paint beacon black. Remove masking tape. Paint catwalk and rails white. Paint base black.

7. Lightly apply wood-tone, then sealer to lighthouse, beacon, catwalk, rail posts, and fence. Apply sealer to base.
8. On back of catwalk, use a pencil to draw four evenly spaced lines from outside edge to inside edge. Place catwalk on lighthouse just below beacon. Mark a dot on lighthouse where each line ends. Remove catwalk. Use awl to punch one small hole in side of lighthouse at each dot. With toothpick ends extending beyond outer edge of catwalk, insert one toothpick horizontally through catwalk at each drawn line. Apply glue to inside edge of catwalk. Replace catwalk on lighthouse. Push toothpicks into lighthouse until toothpick ends are flush with outside edge of catwalk.
9. Drill two holes ¹/₂" apart through flat side of each rail (**Fig. 1**). Spacing evenly, hot glue rail posts onto catwalk. Use needle to thread one length of string through bottom holes and second length of string through top holes; knot at back of lighthouse to secure.

Fig. 1

10. Use hacksaw to cut a 15³/₄" length from pipe stem.
11. Use craft knife to cut a ¹/₂" dia. hole in bottom back of lighthouse. Thread wire down through holes in center of lighthouse, then out hole in back of lighthouse. Wrap end of wire in back of lighthouse around lamp cord. To thread lamp cord, pull wire up through center of lighthouse, then through pipe stem. Thread pipe stem down through holes in lighthouse. Follow manufacturer's instructions to assemble lamp.
12. Glue lighthouse to base. Beginning at back of lamp and keeping electrical cord between fence ends, glue fence around lamp base. Place lampshade on lamp.

CHICKEN COOP

We've hatched the perfect plan for an "**egg-citing**" play room! To make these **colorful** projects, including the **Plucky Chicken Planter**, turn to page 88.

The **Who's Chicken? Toy Box** has a sturdy plastic tub for her frame, so she won't make a peep about holding playroom clutter. For easy projects you can make from "scratch," try the **Restful Roost Bench Cushion** and **"Cheep" Trick Pillows**. What a great place for your little chicks to stretch out for reading or napping!

Kids will be "making tracks" to and from this great **All-Cooped-Up Storage Hutch!** The shelves and baskets can neatly nest lots of playtime necessities in sight, behind the screened doors. It's an easy idea with "egg-cellent" potential. Keep a few jumbo floor pillows at hand for instant seating.

Checkers, anyone? While away the hours with this **"Fowl Play" Table Topper** and count the happy hens on the **"Makin' Tracks" Floor Mat**. For a change, remove the table topper and set out the craft supplies stored in the **Poultry Feeder Tray and Cracked-Up Caddies** shown on page 84.

Any time is fun when the **"Time Almost Flies" Clock** is on watch! Just a few pieces of craft foam turn a plain round wall clock into this reliable feathered friend. When it's movie time, our **Framed Fowl** and the cute little birds painted on the **Video Entertainment Stand** promise not to give away the endings!

87

ALL-COOPED-UP STORAGE HUTCH

(Photo on pg. 85)

SUPPLIES

You will need a wooden hutch; primer; blue latex paint; white, yellow, red, and black acrylic paint; non-toxic spray sealer; non-toxic brush-on sealer; black permanent medium-point marker; 1/4" (23 gauge) hardware screen cloth; wire cutters; staple gun; and baskets with wooden rims to fit on shelves.

INSTRUCTIONS

1. Read **Preparing to Paint** and **Painting**, pg. 110. Paint hutch blue. Paint 1"w white and black stripe along top edge of hutch. Use marker to draw chicken tracks around doors.
2. Paint rims of baskets red or yellow. Apply spray sealer to baskets. Apply brush-on sealer to hutch.
3. Cut screen cloth pieces 1 1/2" larger than door and side openings. Staple cloth to back of door and side openings.

"FOWL PLAY" TABLE TOPPER

(Photo on pg. 86)

SUPPLIES

You will need a vinyl floor covering cut to fit top of table; white gesso; white, yellow, orange, pink, red, and blue acrylic paint; black medium-point and wide-point permanent markers; non-toxic spray sealer; tracing paper; and transfer paper.

Note: Our table topper fits a 20 3/4" x 30 1/4" tabletop. If your tabletop is larger or smaller, you may wish to draw checkerboard center first, then add and adjust borders as room allows.

INSTRUCTIONS

1. Read **Preparing to Paint** and **Painting**, pg. 110. Prime back of floor covering with two coats of gesso; allow to dry. Paint back white.
2. Use pencil to draw a 2"w outer border on all sides of topper, continuing lines to edges of topper. Draw second 4 1/2"w border just inside first border on short ends. For checkerboard, divide center square into sixty-four approx. 2 1/8"w squares.
3. Paint corners of outer border yellow. Paint remainders of outer border red and blue. Paint checkerboard squares red. Use medium-point marker to outline all borders and checkerboard squares with wavy black lines. Use wide-point marker to draw a 1/4"w outer border for checkerboard.
4. Read **Sizing Patterns**, **Tracing Patterns**, and **Transferring Patterns**, pgs. 110 and 111, to reduce chick pattern, pg. 91, to 4"h. Transfer chicks to white borders, reversing pattern if desired. Paint chicks yellow, beaks orange, and cheeks pink. Use medium marker to outline chicks.
5. Trace letter patterns onto tracing paper. Transfer letters to red and blue sections of outer border. Paint letters white. Use medium marker to draw chicken tracks between letters.
6. Paint blue dots on chick border. Apply sealer to topper.

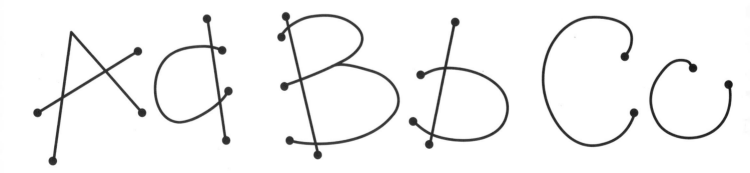

VIDEO ENTERTAINMENT STAND

(Photo on pg. 87)

SUPPLIES

You will need a wooden cabinet; 1/2"w wooden molding; four wooden ball post tops for feet; 1/4" (23 gauge) hardware screen cloth; saw; hammer and nails for post tops; finishing nails for molding; primer; white latex paint; yellow, orange, pink, red, blue, and black acrylic paint; masking tape; tracing paper; transfer paper; non-toxic brush-on sealer; black permanent medium-point marker; wire cutters; and staple gun.

INSTRUCTIONS

1. Nail feet to bottom corners of cabinet. Read **Preparing to Paint** and **Painting**, pg. 110, to prime and paint cabinet and post tops white.

2. Read **Tracing and Transferring Patterns**, pg. 111. Trace chick pattern, pg. 91. Transfer two chicks to front of cabinet, reversing pattern if desired. Paint chicks yellow, beaks orange, and cheeks pink. Use medium-point marker to outline chicks. Paint blue dots on post tops and cabinet front around chicks. Paint 1"w black stripes along side edges of cabinet front. Paint molding, bottom trim of cabinet, and top of cabinet red.

3. Cut a piece of screen cloth to fit over chick designs. Staple screen to cabinet front. Cut molding to fit around edges of screen cloth. Use finishing nails to nail molding to cabinet, covering edges of screen.

4. Apply sealer to cabinet.

POULTRY FEEDER TRAY AND CRACKED-UP CADDIES

(Photo on pg. 84)

SUPPLIES

You will need a metal poultry feeder tray with lid; three 5"h egg-shaped papier-mâché baskets with handles; primer; white, yellow, orange, pink, red, blue, and black acrylic paint; non-toxic spray sealer; tracing paper; transfer paper; and a black permanent fine-point marker.

INSTRUCTIONS

1. Read **Painting**, pg. 110. Apply primer to feeder and eggs. Paint one egg and lid of feeder yellow.

Paint tray of feeder red. Paint interior of tray and lid blue. Paint remaining two eggs white.

2. Read **Sizing Patterns**, pg. 110, to reduce chick pattern, pg. 91, to 4"h. Read **Transferring Patterns**, pg. 111. Transfer pattern to one white egg. Paint chick yellow, beak orange, and cheeks pink. Paint black checks around top and bottom of egg. Paint assorted-size yellow, red, and blue dots on remaining white egg. Paint blue dots around edge of feeder lid. Use marker to outline chick on white egg and draw chicken tracks on yellow egg and feeder lid.

3. Apply sealer to feeder and eggs.

RESTFUL ROOST BENCH CUSHION

(Photo on pg. 84)

SUPPLIES

You will need 2" thick foam cut to fit top of bench, fabric for top of cushion, fabric for bottom of cushion and to cover cord, 3/8" dia. cord, 1 1/2" dia. buttons for cushion top, and 1" dia. buttons for reinforcing.

Note: Use 1/2" seam allowance for all sewing unless otherwise indicated.

INSTRUCTIONS

1. Measure width and length of foam piece; add 5" to each measurement. For cushion cover, cut one piece each from top and bottom fabrics the determined measurements.

2. For cording, measure lengths of one short and one long side of foam; add together and multiply by 2. Cut a length of cord the determined measurement plus 4". Piece fabric as necessary to make a 1 1/2"w bias strip 2" longer than cord. Press one short end 1/2" to wrong side. Center cord on wrong side of bias strip. Fold strip lengthwise over cord and baste long edges together close to cord.

3. Beginning with pressed end of strip, use zipper foot and match raw edges to baste cording to right side of top. Remove 2" of basting on each end of cording. Trim ends of cording to meet exactly. Place raw end inside pressed end. Restitch cording ends to top.

4. Matching right sides and sewing as close to cording as possible, sew top to bottom along one short edge and both long edges. Insert cushion into cover. Hand sew opening closed.

5. With large buttons evenly spaced on top and small buttons directly beneath large buttons on bottom, sew through all layers to secure buttons on cushion.

WHO'S CHICKEN? TOY BOX

(Photo on pg. 84)

SUPPLIES

You will need a 23-gallon round plastic tub with rope handles, two 2 yd lengths and one 1/2 yd length of 45"w fabric, 2 yds of 48"w ultra-loft batting, 3 yds of 3/16" dia. cording, 36" length of 1 1/8" dia. wooden dowel, 14" round knife-edge pillow form, 1/2 yd of 36"w gold felt, 2 yds of 2 1/4"w red satin ribbon, red and black heavy-duty thread, 45" of string, thumbtack, pencil, craft drill, glue gun, white acrylic paint, two 1 1/2" dia. black shank buttons, tracing paper, fusible interfacing, paper-backed fusible web, two 18" lengths of 18 gauge wire, and 3/4" carpet tack.

Note: Use 1/2" seam allowance for all sewing.

INSTRUCTIONS

1. Matching right sides, sew 2 yd lengths of fabric together along one long edge. Press seam open. Read **Cutting a Fabric Circle**, pg. 111, and use a 35" measurement for string to cut a 70" dia. circle for body cover from pieced fabric. Cut two 18" squares from remaining fabric piece. Use a 7 1/2" measurement for string to cut two 14" dia. circles for head cover pieces.

2. Place head cover pieces with right sides together. Leaving an opening large enough to insert pillow form, sew pieces together. Clip seam allowances and turn right side out. Insert pillow form into cover. Make a 1 1/2"w opening in seam of pillow form. Leaving a second 1 1/2"w opening in cover over first, sew opening in cover closed.

3. For neck, cut a 6 1/2" x 18" strip of fabric. Beginning with one short end of strip, wrap strip around end of dowel. Use carpet tack to tack strip to end of dowel (**Fig. 1**). Insert approx. 5" of covered end of dowel into head, angling dowel toward seam (**Fig. 2**). Whipstitch head to neck.

4. Use craft drill to drill two holes in tub 3 1/2" apart and 6" below one rope handle. Drill a second pair of holes directly below first holes and 4" from bottom of tub. Use wire lengths to secure dowel inside tub.

5. Cut one 12" x 72" strip and two 18" x 72" strips of batting. Glue 12" strip around center of tub. Glue 18" strips around tub to cover sides.

6. Open 6" of one end of seam on body cover. Zigzag stitch along opening to reinforce. For drawstring casing, turn under 3/4" on edges of body cover and stitch 1/2" from folded edge. Zigzag stitch seam of casing to reinforce. Thread cording through casing. Center tub on wrong side of body cover. With opening at dowel, pull drawstring to gather cover around tub. Pull drawstring tight and knot ends to secure. Trim drawstring ends.

7. Sew buttons to either side of head at center. Highlight eyes with white paint. For neck feathers, cut two 4 1/2" x 36" pieces of felt. Make 2 1/2" deep cuts in varying widths along one long edge of each piece. Clip ends of "feathers" into points. Glue neck feathers around dowel between head and body.

8. Trace beak top and beak bottom patterns. Cut one beak top and beak bottom piece each from interfacing and web. Cut two beak tops and two beak bottoms from felt. For beak top, fuse interfacing to one felt piece and web to remaining felt piece. Repeat for beak bottom. Matching edges, fuse web-covered pieces to interfaced pieces. Glue beak top to head. Glue beak bottom to beak top and head.

9. Cut five 12" lengths of ribbon. Sew ends of three ribbons to head for comb and two ribbons to head for wattle.

Beak Top

Beak Bottom

Fig. 1

Fig. 2

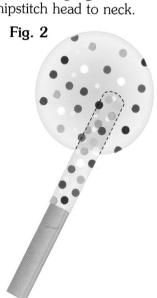

90

"MAKIN' TRACKS" FLOOR MAT

(Photo on pg. 86)

SUPPLIES

You will need a 46" x 52" piece of vinyl floor covering; white gesso; white, yellow, orange, pink, red, and blue acrylic paint; black medium-point and wide-point permanent markers; non-toxic brush-on sealer; tracing paper; and transfer paper.

INSTRUCTIONS

1. Read **Preparing to Paint** and **Painting**, pg. 110. Prime back of floor covering with two coats of gesso; allow to dry. Paint back white.
2. Use pencil to draw a $2^1/4$"w outer border on all sides of mat. Draw a $^5/8$"w second border and a $^3/8$"w third border just inside first border. Draw a 2"w border $8^3/4$" from third border.
3. Paint first border red and second border yellow. Paint center rectangle of mat yellow. Paint 2"w border blue. Use medium-point marker to outline all borders with wavy black lines. Use wide-point marker to make black stripes on $^3/8$"w border.
4. Read **Sizing Patterns**, **Tracing Patterns**, and **Transferring Patterns**, pgs. 110 and 111. Reduce chick pattern to $5^3/4$"h. Transfer chicks to mat between striped and blue borders, reversing pattern for two of the chicks. Paint chicks. Use medium marker to outline chicks and draw chicken tracks between chicks and in center of mat.
5. Paint blue dots on chick border. Apply sealer to mat.

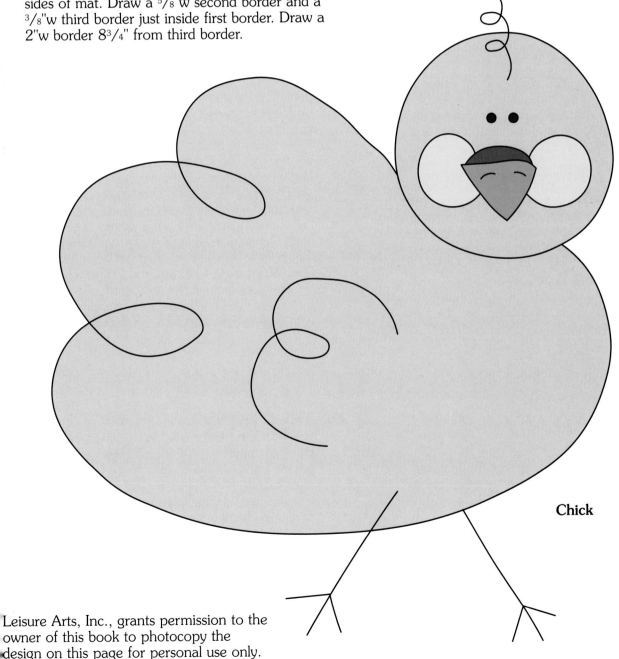

Chick

Leisure Arts, Inc., grants permission to the owner of this book to photocopy the design on this page for personal use only.

"CHEEP" TRICK PILLOWS

(Photo on pg. 84)

SUPPLIES

For each large pillow, you will need a 26" square knife-edge pillow form, 24" of 1"w hook and loop fastener tape, and a 27" x 58" piece of fabric.

For each small pillow, you will need an 18" square knife-edge pillow form, 16" of $1/2$"w hook and loop fastener tape, and a 19" x 42" piece of fabric.

INSTRUCTIONS

1. For pillow cover, press short edges $1/2$", then 1" to wrong side; topstitch to secure.
2. Pull fastener pieces apart. Sew one fastener piece along one short edge of cover on wrong side. Sew remaining piece along remaining short edge on right side. Overlapping ends 1", use fingers to press fastener strips together.
3. Turn cover wrong side out. With overlapped ends at center back, use $1/2$" seam allowance to sew sides of cover together; clip corners. Open fasteners; turn right side out. Insert form into cover.

FRAMED FOWL

(Photo on pg. 87)

SUPPLIES

You will need a 14" x 17" piece of poster board, frame with $15^1/2$" x $19^1/2$" opening, white mat board to fit frame, pencil, ruler, tracing paper, transfer paper, black permanent medium-point and wide-point markers, colored pencils, sawtooth hanger kit, hammer, blue acrylic paint, non-toxic spray sealer, and spray adhesive.

INSTRUCTIONS

1. Use pencil to draw a 1"w outer border on all sides of poster board, continuing lines to edges of board. Draw a second $1/2$"w border just inside outer border. Draw third $2^1/4$"w border just inside second border on short ends only.
2. Read **Sizing Patterns**, **Tracing Patterns**, and **Transferring Patterns**, pgs. 110 and 111, to enlarge chick pattern, pg. 91, to 8"h. Transfer chick design to center of poster board, reversing pattern if desired. Trace letter patterns, pg. 88, onto tracing paper. Transfer letters to $2^1/4$"w borders.
3. Draw chicken tracks on long sections of outer borders. Divide second border into $1/2$" squares. Draw dots on chick background. Draw over letters with wide-point marker. Draw over all other drawn and transferred lines with medium-point marker.
4. Use colored pencils to color poster board. Spray back of poster with spray adhesive. Glue poster to mat board.
5. Read **Preparing to Paint** and **Painting**, pg. 110. Follow manufacturer's instructions to attach hanger to back of frame. Paint frame blue. Spray frame with sealer. Glue mat board in frame.

"TIME ALMOST FLIES" CLOCK

(Photo on pg. 87)

SUPPLIES

You will need tracing paper; 8" dia. white clock; white, orange, and red craft foam; $1/2$" dia. black button; and a low-temperature glue gun.

INSTRUCTIONS

1. Read **Tracing Patterns**, pg. 111. Trace clock chicken patterns, pgs. 92 and 93, onto tracing paper. Use patterns to cut chicken pieces from craft foam.
2. Glue chicken pieces together. Glue chicken pieces to clock. Glue button to chicken for eye.

Head

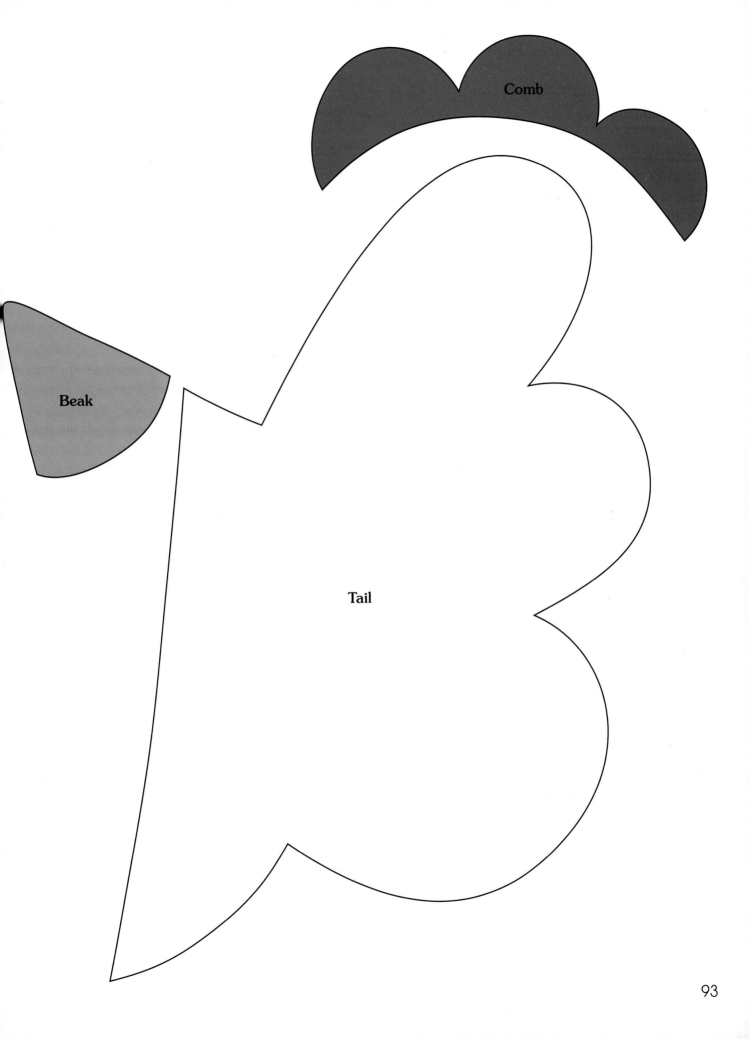

Comb

Beak

Tail

PLUCKY CHICKEN PLANTER

(Photo on pg. 82)

SUPPLIES

You will need a one-gallon plastic bottle, craft knife, cutting mat, $3/4$ yd of muslin, string, thumbtack, pencil, polyester fiberfill, glue gun, tracing paper, $1/4$ yd each of gold and red fabrics, wooden skewer, soft sculpture needle, two $7/8$" dia. black buttons, cosmetic blush powder, and two 12" lengths of jute twine.

Note: Match right sides and use a $1/4$" seam allowance for all sewing unless otherwise indicated.

INSTRUCTIONS

1. Mark around bottle 7" from bottom. Use craft knife to cut top from bottle; discard top.
2. For body, cut a 26" square piece from muslin. Follow **Cutting a Fabric Circle**, pg. 111, and use 12" for string measurement to cut a 24" dia. circle from muslin. Baste around circle $1/4$" from edge. Place bottle piece in center of circle. Pull thread ends, filling space between muslin and bottle with fiberfill while gathering muslin. Tighten muslin around top edge of bottle; knot thread ends to secure. Glue gathers inside bottle to secure.
3. Read **Tracing Patterns**, pg. 111. Trace patterns, pgs. 94 and 95. Use patterns to cut two heads and four each of wings and feet from muslin, two combs and two wattles from red fabric, and two beaks from gold fabric. Cut two 3" x 20" strips from gold fabric for legs. Cut one 2" x 18" and one 3" x 18" piece from gold fabric for collar.
4. For head, match raw edges of beak pieces and sew along two edges. Turn beak right side out and lightly stuff with fiberfill. Matching raw edges, pin beak to right side of one head piece where indicated on pattern. Leaving bottom open, sew head pieces together.

Turn head right side out. Leaving a 5" tail of thread at beginning and end, baste around bottom of head $1/8$" from edge. Stuff head with fiberfill. Insert skewer in bottom of head. Pull thread ends to tightly gather bottom of head around skewer; knot thread ends to secure, then trim ends. Glue skewer to inside of bottle to secure.

5. Leaving an opening for turning, sew comb pieces together. Turn comb right side out. Stuff comb with fiberfill. Sew opening closed. Leaving an opening for turning, sew wattle pieces together. Turn wattle right side out. Stuff wattle with fiberfill. Sew opening closed. Glue comb and wattle to head. Use soft sculpture needle to sew on buttons for eyes. Apply blush for cheeks.
6. For collar, with right sides up and aligning one long edge, place 2" x 18" collar piece on top of 3" x 18" collar piece. Leaving a 5" tail of thread at beginning and end, baste along aligned edges. To fringe collar, clip collar pieces at $1/2$" intervals to $1/4$" from basting threads. Place collar around neck. Pull thread ends to gather collar; knot to secure.
7. For each wing, leaving an opening for turning, sew two wing pieces together. Turn wing right side out. Stuff wing with fiberfill. Sew opening closed. Glue wings to sides of body.
8. For each leg, matching long edges, fold one leg strip in half. Sew along long edges of strip. Turn right side out. Thread one length of twine through strip. Sewing at open ends to secure, gather strip to fit twine.
9. For each foot, leaving an opening for turning, sew two feet pieces together. Turn foot right side out. Stuff foot with fiberfill. Sew opening closed. Glue feet to ends of legs. Glue opposite ends of legs to body.

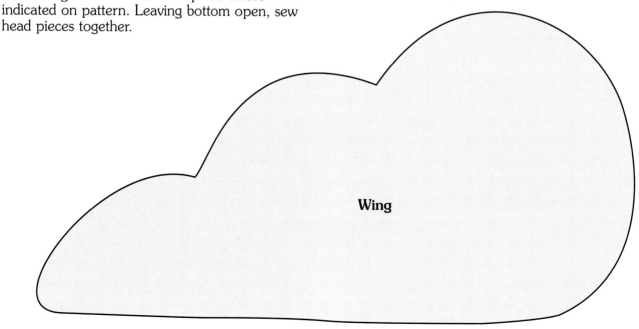

Wing

94

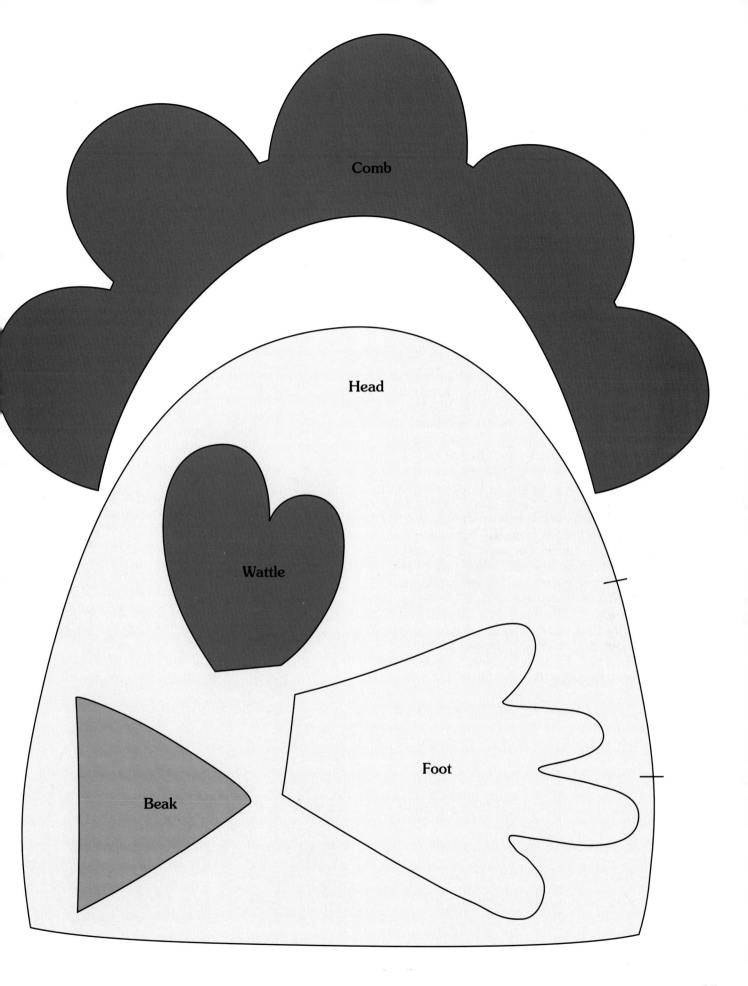

Comb

Head

Wattle

Beak

Foot

MEMORY LANE

With a click of her **ruby slippers**, your little girl will travel back to the childhood of yesteryear in this nostalgic room! The **Chenille Lamp**, with its hobnail milk-glass base, begins our walk down a very special memory lane. Instructions begin on page 102.

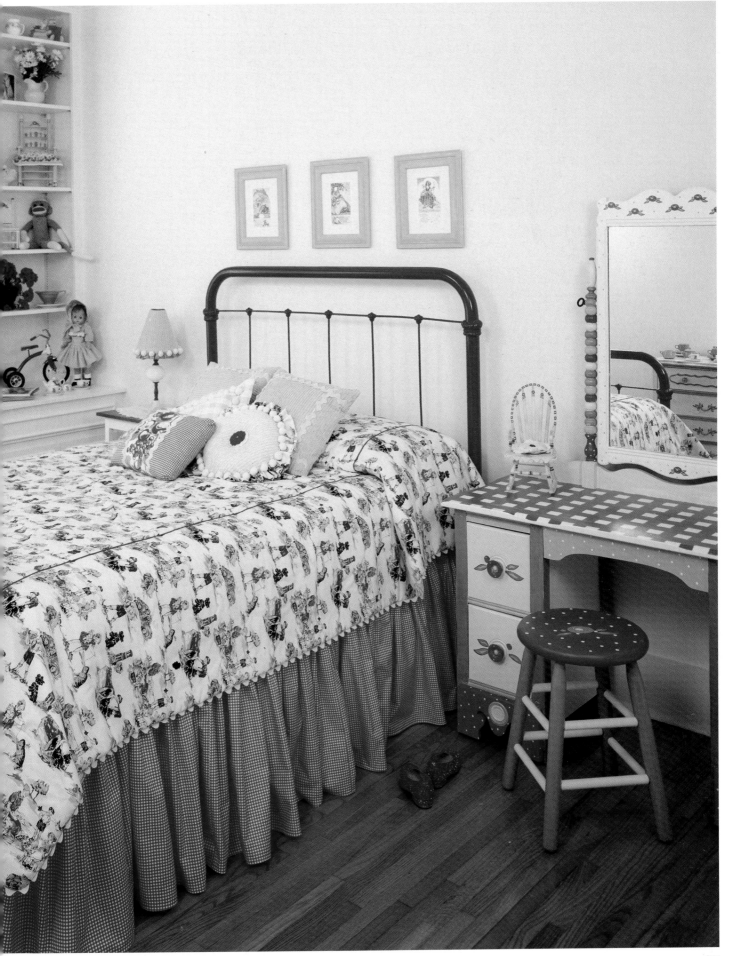

The best looks of the good old days will never go out of style! Revive worn furniture as a **Retro Dresser and Stool** with sweetly painted posies and red "gingham" checks. The cute pint-size **Storybook Table and Chairs** are just right for tea parties, and it's child's play to make extra doll chairs for toy-room friends, too!

Unpack Grandma's vintage linens to make great new room accessories like the **Retro Tablecloth Valance**. **Mom's Apron Toy Holder** features jumbo pockets fashioned from dish towels.

Combine flea market finds with reproduction "nostalgia" fabrics to make plump pillows. Loved by generations of beginning readers, the familiar characters printed on the **Good Old Days Comforter** will find a new friend in your little girl. For more of that fabulous Fifties feel, skirt the bed in a bright **Gingham Dust Ruffle**. Decorating has never been so elementary!

101

RETRO TABLECLOTH VALANCE

(Photo, pg. 100)

SUPPLIES
You will need a 3"w valance rod to fit window, one or more square or rectangular vintage tablecloth(s) with a wide border print (we used one 68" long tablecloth), gingham fabric, and 1½"w pom-pom fringe.

Note: Match right sides and use a ¼" seam allowance unless otherwise indicated.

INSTRUCTIONS
1. Measure width of window; multiply by 2.5 for finished length of valance.
2. For valance, cut tablecloth(s) in half lengthwise. Trim short ends of one or more halves so that total length of all tablecloth pieces equals finished length of valance. Sew halves together along short ends.
3. For rod pocket, cut a 7½"w piece of gingham fabric same length as valance plus 1". Press short ends ½" to wrong side; topstitch to secure. Press one long edge ½" to wrong side.
4. Sew long raw edge of rod pocket to top edge of valance. Press pocket toward seam allowance.
5. With remaining long edge of rod pocket overlapping valance ¼", fold rod pocket to wrong side of valance. Topstitch pressed edge to secure pocket to valance.
6. For hem, cut a 5"w piece of gingham fabric 1" longer than valance. Press short ends under ½"; sew in place. Press long edges ½" to wrong side. Matching wrong sides, press hem in half lengthwise.
7. Insert bottom edge of valance inside fold of hem. Sew along pressed edges to secure hem to valance. Cut fringe same length as valance. Sew fringe to hem.
8. Follow valance rod manufacturer's instructions to install valance.

FLANGED SEERSUCKER PILLOW

(Photo, pg. 101)

SUPPLIES
You will need two 17½" squares of yellow checked seersucker, 12" square knife-edge pillow form, and 1½ yds of 1½"w pom-pom fringe.

Note: Match right sides and use a ½" seam allowance unless otherwise indicated.

INSTRUCTIONS
1. Press one edge of each fabric square ½" to wrong side. Matching pressed edges, sew squares together along raw edges. Clip corners and turn pillow right side out; press.
2. Beginning and ending 2¼" from open end, topstitch top edge of fringe 2¼" from sewn edges of pillow, folding fringe at corners as necessary; do not cut fringe.
3. Insert pillow form into pillow. Overlapping fringe ends, topstitch top edge of fringe 2¼" from open end. Trim away excess fringe. To secure fringe, topstitch a second time ½" from first topstitching. Hand sew opening closed.

ROUND YELLOW CHENILLE PILLOW

(Photo, pg. 101)

SUPPLIES

You will need two 15" squares of yellow chenille fabric, 12" round knife-edge pillow form, string, thumbtack, fabric marking pen, $1/2$ yd of 45"w print fabric, $1^1/4$ yds of $1^1/2$"w pom-pom fringe, $2^1/2$" dia. covered button kit, 1" yellow button, heavy-duty thread, and a $4^1/2$" dia. or larger crocheted doily.

Note: Match right sides and use a $1/2$" seam allowance unless otherwise indicated.

INSTRUCTIONS

1. Read **Cutting a Fabric Circle**, pg. 111, and use a $6^1/2$" measurement for string to cut two 13" dia. circles from chenille squares.
2. Trimming ends to fit, pin top edge of fringe along edge of one circle.
3. For ruffle, cut three 5" x 42" strips from print fabric. Sew short ends of strips together; trim to 102" long, setting remaining fabric aside. Press one short end $1/2$" to wrong side. Matching wrong sides, press strip in half lengthwise. Use a $1/4$" seam allowance to baste along long raw edges.
4. Matching raw edges and overlapping ends 2", pull basting threads, gathering strip to fit circle. Pin ruffle to right side of circle over fringe. Use $1/4$" seam allowance to baste ruffle to circle, leaving 2" of ruffle ends free. Remove gathering thread from approx. 2" of folded end. Insert raw end into folded end. Baste ends to circle. Hand sew opening in ruffle closed.
5. Leaving an opening for turning, sew circles together. Turn pillow right side out. Place form in pillow. Hand sew opening closed.
6. Cut a 5" square from print fabric. Follow manufacturer's instructions to cover $2^1/2$" dia. button with print fabric.
7. Place covered button upside down on center back of doily. Baste around edge of doily. Pull thread ends to gather doily around button; tie to secure.
8. With 1" button on center back of pillow for support and using heavy-duty thread, sew through all layers to secure covered button to center front of pillow.

RED GINGHAM RECTANGLE PILLOW

(Photo, pg. 101)

SUPPLIES

You will need one 13" x 17" and two $5^3/4$" x 13" pieces of red gingham fabric, one $7^1/2$" x 13" piece from a vintage print tablecloth, two 13" lengths of yellow jumbo rickrack, clear nylon thread, and polyester fiberfill.

Note: Match right sides and use a $1/2$" seam allowance unless otherwise indicated.

INSTRUCTIONS

1. For pillow front, match long edges and sew one small gingham piece to each side of vintage print piece. Press seams toward gingham.
2. Use a wide zigzag stitch to topstitch a length of rickrack over each seam on pillow front.
3. Leaving an opening for turning, sew pillow front to remaining fabric piece. Baste a diagonal line $1^1/2$" away from each corner (**Fig. 1**). Pull thread ends to gather each corner. Sew over gathers to secure.

Fig. 1

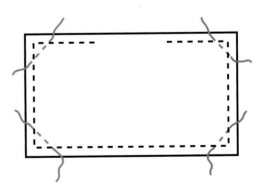

4. Clip corners and turn pillow right side out. Stuff with fiberfill; hand sew opening closed.

BLUE CHENILLE SQUARE PILLOW

(Photo, pg. 101)

SUPPLIES

You will need two 17" squares of blue chenille fabric, 16" square knife-edge pillow form, clear nylon thread, and four 17" lengths of yellow jumbo rickrack.

Note: Match right sides and use a $1/2$" seam allowance unless otherwise indicated.

INSTRUCTIONS

1. Use a wide zigzag stitch to topstitch a length of rickrack $3\frac{1}{2}$" from each edge of one square.
2. Sew three sides of squares together; clip corners. Turn pillow right side out. Insert pillow form into pillow. Hand sew opening closed.

MOM'S APRON TOY HOLDER

(Photo, pg. 100)

SUPPLIES

You will need $1\frac{1}{4}$ yds of 44"w border print fabric (ours has a rickrack design), 14" x 28" vintage embroidered table runner, and two 8" square lace-edged handkerchiefs.

INSTRUCTIONS

1. With border at one long edge, cut one $28\frac{1}{2}$" x 40" fabric piece for skirt. Cut one 5" x 20" piece for waist and two 3" x 39" pieces for ties.
2. For pockets, matching short edges, fold table runner in half; cut along fold. Fold handkerchiefs in half diagonally; cut along folds. Matching raw edges and overlapping as necessary to fit pocket, pin two handkerchief pieces to top edge of each pocket. Press top edge of pockets $1/2$" to wrong sides; topstitch to secure. Pin each pocket to front of skirt 2" above border print and 4" from side. Topstitch sides and bottoms of pockets to secure.
3. Press one short edge and both long edges of apron ties $1/4$" to wrong side twice; topstitch to secure.
4. Press bottom edge of skirt $1/4$" to wrong side twice; topstitch to secure. Repeat to press and sew sides of skirt.
5. To gather skirt, baste $1/4$" from top edge. Pulling thread ends, gather top of skirt to 19"; tie thread ends to secure.
6. Press short edges and one long edge of waist $1/2$" to wrong side; topstitch to secure. Matching right sides and raw edges and using $1/2$" seam allowance, sew waist to top of skirt. Press seam allowance toward waist. Matching wrong sides, fold waist in half lengthwise. Leaving short ends open, hand sew remaining long edge to back of skirt.
7. Insert $1/2$" of unfinished end of each tie into an opening in waist. Topstitch to secure.

CHENILLE LAMP

(Photo, pg. 96)

SUPPLIES

You will need a lamp with shade, red gingham and blue chenille fabrics, pom-pom fringe, tissue paper, spray adhesive, glue gun, red acrylic paint, non-toxic brush-on sealer, and primer.

INSTRUCTIONS

1. If your lamp has wooden sections, read **Preparing to Paint** and **Painting**, pg. 110, to prime and paint red trim on lamp base. Apply sealer to lamp base. Paint top 1/2" of lampshade red.
2. Read **Covering a Lampshade**, pg. 111, to cover lampshade with chenille fabric. Glue a length of fringe around inside bottom of shade.
3. For ruffle, measure around bottom of lampshade; multiply by 2.5. Cut a 5"w piece of gingham fabric the determined measurement. Press short edges 1/2" to wrong side. Matching wrong sides, fold in half lengthwise. Baste 1/4" from raw edges. Pull basting threads, gathering ruffle to fit around inside bottom of shade. Glue ruffle inside lampshade.

STRAIGHT-BACKED DOLL CHAIRS

(Photo, pg. 99)

SUPPLIES

You will need two 11¼"h wooden chairs; primer; tracing paper; transfer paper; white latex paint; small sponge; glazing medium; light yellow, yellow, red, blue, light green, green, and black acrylic paint; non-toxic spray sealer; and any additional supplies listed in General Instructions (see Step 1).

Note: Instructions are for one chair.

INSTRUCTIONS

1. Read **Preparing to Paint**, **Painting**, **Painting Details**, and **Transferring Patterns**, pgs. 110 and 111.
2. Prepare chair for painting. Paint chair light green. Mix one part white paint to one part glazing medium. Sponge paint mixture over all surfaces of chair.
3. Paint tops of uprights, bottoms of chair legs, and top edge of chair back red. Paint red stripes on bottom of chair back, front and sides of seat, and front of chair legs. Outline back of chair with red dots and add red dots to chair legs. Add yellow dots to red dots on legs.
4. Transfer small flower pattern, pg. 107, to chair back. Outline design in blue. Paint design according to pattern. Outline design in black. Apply sealer to chair.

GINGHAM DUST RUFFLE

(Photo, pg. 101)

SUPPLIES

You will need gingham fabric for skirt, 1"w gathering tape, and large safety pins.

Note: Dust ruffle is three finished pieces.

INSTRUCTIONS

1. To determine height of all dust ruffle pieces, measure from floor to top of box springs; add 2". For length of foot piece, measure width of box springs at foot; multiply by 2.5. For length of each side piece, measure side of box springs; multiply by 2.5. Piecing fabric as necessary, cut one foot piece and two side pieces.

2. Press short edges of each piece $1/4$" to wrong side twice; topstitch to secure. For hem, press one long edge of each piece $1/4$" to wrong side twice; topstitch to secure. For top edge of each piece, press remaining long edges $3/4$" to wrong side twice; topstitch to secure.

3. Follow manufacturer's instructions to sew gathering tape along wrong side of top edge of each dust ruffle piece. Pull strings, gathering ruffles to fit box springs; knot or tie strings to secure. Use safety pins to pin gathered edges of dust ruffles to top of box springs.

STORYBOOK TABLE AND CHAIRS

(Photo, pg. 99)

SUPPLIES

You will need a child's wooden table and chairs; primer; white latex paint; light yellow, yellow, red, blue, light green, green, and black acrylic paint; glazing medium; tracing paper; transfer paper; non-toxic brush-on sealer; soft cloth; and any additional supplies listed in General Instructions (see Step 1).

INSTRUCTIONS

1. Read **Preparing to Paint**, **Painting**, **Painting Details**, and **Transferring Patterns**, pgs. 110 and 111.

2. Prepare table and chairs for painting. Paint table and chairs white. Paint top of table and chair seats light green. Paint leg rungs, curved upright of chair back, and edge of tabletop red. Paint sections of chair back spindles and tops of chair legs as desired. Shade table skirt and tops of table legs with blue paint to imitate bottom edge and folds of a tablecloth. Paint red dots along bottom edge of shading.

3. Transfer desired size flower pattern, pg. 107, to tabletop. Paint designs according to patterns. Outline designs with black paint.

4. For whitewash, mix one part white paint to one part glazing medium. Working on small sections, paint mixture onto table and chairs and wipe off with soft cloth.

5. Apply sealer to table and chairs.

RETRO DRESSER AND STOOL

Photo, pg. 98)

SUPPLIES

You will need a wooden dresser; a wooden stool; rimer; tracing paper; transfer paper; white latex paint; white, light yellow, yellow, red, blue, light green, green, and black acrylic paint; glazing medium; non-toxic rush-on sealer; 2"w flat brush; and any additional supplies listed in General Instructions, (see Step 1).

INSTRUCTIONS

1. Read **Preparing to Paint**, **Painting**, **Painting Details**, and **Transferring Patterns**, pgs. 110 and 111.
2. Prepare dresser and stool for painting. Paint dresser and mirror frame white. Refer to photo to paint portions of dresser and stool yellow, blue, green, and red. Using a 2"w flat brush for best results, begin in centers of top and sides to paint red stripes on dresser.

3. Transfer leaves from large flower pattern to drawer fronts. Transfer large flower pattern to sides of dresser and top of stool. Transfer small flower pattern to mirror frame. Paint designs according to patterns. Paint drawer pulls red with yellow centers and highlights. Outline transferred designs with black paint. Paint yellow dots on red areas of dresser and stool. Paint blue dots on mirror frame. Paint white dots on blue skirt.
4. For whitewash, mix one part white paint to one part glazing medium. Working on small sections, paint mixture onto dresser and wipe off with soft cloth.
5. Apply sealer to dresser and stool.

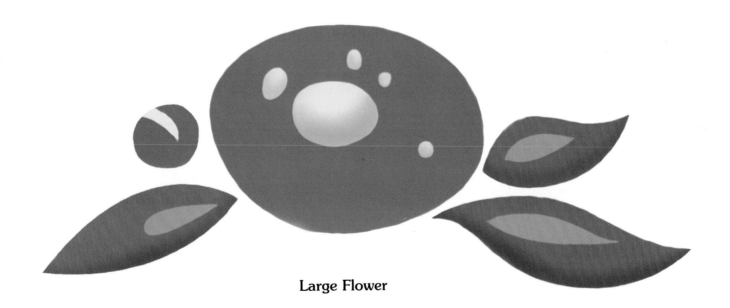

Large Flower

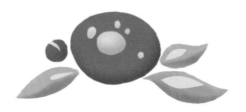

Small Flower

LADDER-BACK DOLL CHAIR WITH CUSHION

(Photo, pg. 99)

SUPPLIES

You will need a 15½"h wooden chair; primer; tracing paper; transfer paper; white, light yellow, yellow, red, blue, light green, green, and black acrylic paint; glazing medium; non-toxic spray sealer; soft cloth; 11" square handkerchief; 8" square of fabric for backing; scrap of yellow fabric; ⅞" dia. covered button kit; ¼" dia. button; heavy-duty thread; polyester fiberfill; and any additional supplies listed in General Instructions (see Step 1).

Note: Match right sides and use a ½" seam allowance unless otherwise indicated.

INSTRUCTIONS

1. Read **Preparing to Paint, Painting, Painting Details,** and **Transferring Patterns,** pgs. 110 and 111.
2. Prepare chair for painting. Paint chair blue. Paint tops of uprights and chair back rungs yellow. Paint sections of uprights, legs, and lower rungs green. Paint yellow dots on sides of arms and around bottom of legs.
3. Transfer small flower pattern, pg. 107, to top chair back rung. Paint design according to pattern. Outline design in black.
4. Thin red and yellow paint using one part paint to one part glazing medium. Use yellow mixture to paint plaid pattern over green sections of uprights and chair legs. Use red and yellow mixtures to paint plaid design on lower rungs of chair back.
5. For whitewash, mix one part white paint to one part glazing medium. Working on small sections, paint mixture onto chair and wipe off with soft cloth.
6. Apply sealer to chair.
7. For cushion, press edges of 8" fabric square ¼" to wrong side. Matching wrong sides, center and pin 8" square on handkerchief. Leaving an opening for stuffing, topstitch along edges of 8" square. Stuff cushion with fiberfill. Sew opening closed.
8. Follow manufacturer's instructions to cover ⅞" dia. button with yellow fabric. Using heavy-duty thread and sewing through ¼" dia. button at back of cushion, sew through all layers to secure covered button to center front of cushion.

RICKRACK DOLL ROCKER WITH CUSHION

(Photo, pg. 99)

SUPPLIES

You will need a 12½"h wooden rocking chair; primer; white latex paint; glazing medium; white, yellow, and red acrylic paint; wood-tone spray; non-toxic spray sealer; yellow jumbo rickrack; glue gun; two 6" dia. doilies; two 5" squares of blue fabric; drawing compass; pinking shears; ¾" dia. blue shank button; ¼" dia. button to match doilies; polyester fiberfill; and any additional supplies listed in General Instructions (see Step 1).

INSTRUCTIONS

1. Read **Preparing to Paint, Painting,** and **Painting Details,** pg. 110.
2. Prepare chair for painting. Mix one part white paint to one part glazing medium. Brush one coat of mixture over all surfaces of chair. Lightly spray chair with wood-tone spray.
3. Paint one large yellow dot at the top of each chair back spindle. Paint desired sections of arm spindles, legs, and leg rung red. Paint red stripes along curve of chair back. Use red paint to make dot flowers on top of yellow dots. Paint white dots on red sections and stripes.
4. Apply sealer to chair.
5. Fold rickrack in half lengthwise. Glue fold to seat, overlapping and trimming ends at back of chair.
6. Use compass to draw two 5" circles on fabric squares. Use pinking shears to cut out circles. Matching wrong sides and leaving an opening for stuffing, sew circles together ¼" from edge.
7. Matching wrong sides of doilies, place fabric circles between doilies. Leaving a second opening for stuffing beside first opening, sew around cushion 1" from edge of doilies. Stuff cushion with fiberfill. Sew openings closed.
8. Sewing through ¼" dia. button at back of cushion, sew through all layers to secure shank button to center front of cushion.

GOOD OLD DAYS COMFORTER

(Photo, pg. 101)

SUPPLIES

For full-size comforter shown, you will need $6^1/_3$ yds of 44"w fabric for top, one 79" x 110" piece each of batting and fabric for backing (pieced if necessary), $6^1/_4$ yds of flanged piping, 7" dia. salad plate, fabric marking pen, and $8^1/_2$ yds of jumbo (1"w) rickrack.

Note: Match right sides and use a $^1/_2$" seam allowance unless otherwise indicated.

INSTRUCTIONS

1. For center panel of comforter top, cut a piece of print fabric 43" x 110". For side panels, cut two pieces of print fabric 19" x 110". Cut two 110" lengths of piping.
2. Matching raw edges, baste one length of piping to each long edge on right side of center panel. Matching long edges, pin side panels to center panel. Using a zipper foot on sewing machine and stitching as close to piping as possible, sew side panels to center panel. Press seam allowances toward side panels. Topstitch seam allowances $^1/_4$" from piping.
3. Draw around curve of plate to round bottom corners of comforter top (Fig. 2). Cut along drawn lines.

Fig. 2

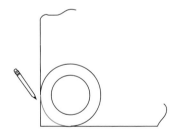

4. With ends of rickrack even with top edge, baste rickrack to right side of comforter top along side and bottom edges.
5. With edges even, pin batting to wrong side of top. Baste batting to top along all edges.
6. Pin top to backing. Leaving an opening for turning, sew comforter together through all layers. Turn comforter right side out. Sew opening closed. Baste through all layers of comforter from center to corners and sides.
7. Set sewing machine on buttonhole stitch with very short stitch length. To tack layers together, sew $^1/_2$" long rows of stitches 12" to 14" apart over all of comforter. Remove basting threads.

For twin-size comforter, you will need $6^1/_3$ yds of 44"w fabric for top, one 70" x 110" piece each of batting and fabric for backing (pieced if necessary), $6^1/_4$ yds of flanged piping, 7" dia. salad plate, and $8^1/_4$ yds of jumbo (1"w) rickrack.

To make a comforter for a twin-size mattress, cut center panel of comforter top 40" x 110" and side panels 16" x 110". Cut two 110" lengths of piping. Follow Steps 2 - 7 of Good Old Days Comforter to make comforter.

GENERAL INSTRUCTIONS

Preparing to Paint

For safety's sake, carefully follow all manufacturers' instructions and warnings when using any cleaning, stripping, painting, or finishing product. Use only non-toxic primers, paints, and sealers that are recommended for children's furniture.

You may need household cleaner, oil soap, sponges, soft cloths, old paintbrush, toothbrush, paint/varnish stripper, wood putty, putty knife, wire brush, assorted grit or gauge sandpaper or steel wool, tack cloth, and items for repairing furniture (hammer, screwdriver, drill, nails, screws, clamps, wood glue).

Preparation

Before you paint, the item to be painted should be in working condition, clean, and ready to accept paint.

1. Clean furniture. Remove any upholstered pieces if needed. Remove surface grime by cleaning with a non-abrasive cleaner such as oil soap.
2. Remove hardware and prepare surface. The type of finish currently on your furniture determines preparations.

   Unfinished Wood or
   Finished Wood in Good Condition
   Use fine-grit sandpaper to lightly sand entire surface.

   Finished Wood in Poor Condition
   Knock off peeling or chipping paint with a wire brush. If surface is lumpy or shows brush strokes due to multiple layers of paint, use paint stripper to strip paint from surface. Smooth rough areas with medium-grit sandpaper, then lightly sand entire piece with fine-grit sandpaper.
3. Make repairs.
4. Wipe down furniture using a tack cloth to remove dust.

Painting

You may need masking tape, Kraft paper or newspaper, waxed paper, primer, paint, sealer (suggested in individual instructions or of your choice), and paintbrushes.

Note: Allow primer, paint, glazing medium, stain, wash, and sealer to dry after each application unless otherwise indicated.

1. Mask off any area you don't wish to paint. Use masking tape and Kraft paper as needed.

2. Unless project instructions indicate otherwise, apply a primer to your prepared surface before painting.
3. In most cases, you will need to paint the entire piece of furniture a single background color before you add details. Apply paint using a paintbrush designed for the type of paint you are using, or you may use spray paint. Both types of paint may require more than one coat for even coverage.
4. Follow individual project instructions to paint details.

Sealing

Follow sealer manufacturer's instructions to seal small objects, such as doll chairs and lamp bases, with a spray sealer. To seal large objects, such as furniture and shelves, use a brush-on sealer. Apply at least 2-3 coats; allow to dry after each application.

Painting Details

Dots

Dip the handle end of a paintbrush into paint. Touch end of paintbrush handle to surface.

Dot Flowers

Make a circle of dots. Add a dot in center of flower.

Shading and Highlighting

Dip flat paintbrush into water; blot on paper towel. Dip corner of paintbrush into paint. Stroke on waxed paper a few times to blend paint into brush. Stroke paintbrush on area to be shaded or highlighted.

Sponge Painting

Lightly dip sponge into paint. Blot sponge on paper towel to remove excess paint. Press sponge onto surface; lift sponge straight up.

Sizing Patterns

Divide desired height or width (whichever is largest) of pattern by the present height or width of pattern. Multiply the result by 100%. Photocopy the pattern at this percentage.

For example: You want your pattern to be 8" high, but the pattern on the page is 6" high.
So, 8 ÷ 6 = 1.33 and 1.33 x 100% = 133%.
You would copy the pattern at 133%.

Tracing Patterns

When one half of pattern (indicated by dashed line on pattern) is shown, fold tracing paper or tissue paper in half and place fold along dashed line of pattern. Trace pattern half; turn folded paper over and draw over all markings. Unfold pattern and lay flat. Cut out pattern. To reverse a pattern, trace pattern onto tracing paper. Turn pattern over and draw over lines on back of pattern.

Transferring Patterns

You will need tracing paper, transfer paper, and a dull pencil.

Trace pattern onto tracing paper. Position tracing paper on surface; slide transfer paper between tracing paper and surface. Use a dull pencil to trace over all lines of the pattern.

Covering A Lampshade

1. To make pattern, find seamline of lampshade. If shade does not have a seamline, draw a vertical line from top edge to bottom edge of shade.
2. Center tissue paper edge on shade seamline, tape in place. Wrap paper around shade extending 1" past seamline; tape to secure (**Fig. 1**).

Fig. 1

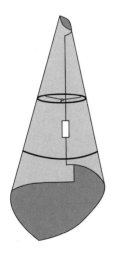

3. Trace along top and bottom edges of shade. Draw a vertical line from top edge to bottom edge of shade 1" past seamline. Remove paper, cut along drawn lines.
4. Use pattern to cut cover from desired fabric or paper.
5. Fold one straight edge of cover $1/2$" to wrong side; press.
6. Matching unpressed straight edge of cover to seamline, use spray adhesive to apply cover to shade. Use glue to secure pressed edge.

Cutting a Fabric Circle

1. Matching right sides, fold fabric square(s) in half from top to bottom and again from left to right.
2. Tie one end of a length of string to a fabric marking pen. Measuring from pen, insert a thumbtack through string at length from pencil indicated in project instructions. Insert thumbtack through folded corner of fabric. Holding tack in place and keeping string taut, mark cutting line (**Fig. 1**). If a second measurement is given, repeat to mark second cutting line.

Fig. 1

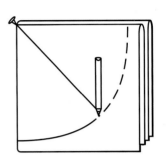

3. Cut along drawn lines through all fabric layers; unfold circle.

Embroidery Stitches

Use 2 to 3 strands of floss for all embroidering unless otherwise indicated in project instructions.

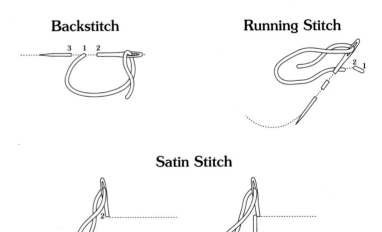

Backstitch

Running Stitch

Satin Stitch

EDITORIAL STAFF

Vice President and Editor-in-Chief:
Anne Van Wagner Childs
Executive Director: Sandra Graham Case
Design Director: Cyndi Hansen
Editorial Director: Susan Frantz Wiles
Publications Director: Susan White Sullivan
Creative Art Director: Gloria Bearden
Art Operations Director: Jeff Curtis

DESIGN
Senior Designer: Sandra Spotts Ritchie
Designers: Polly Tullis Browning, Diana Sanders Cates,
Cherece Athy Cooper, Billie Steward, Anne Pulliam
Stocks, and Linda Diehl Tiano
Executive Assistant: Debra Smith

TECHNICAL
Managing Editors: Beth Knife and Celia Fahr Harkey
Technical Writer: Susan McManus Johnson
Technical Associates: Heather Doyal, Susan Frazier,
Laura Siar Holyfield, Kim Smith, and Theresa Young

EDITORIAL
Managing Editor: Tammi Williamson Bradley
Editorial Writer: Susan McManus Johnson

ART
Senior Art Director: Rhonda Hodge Shelby
Art Director/Color Technician: Mark Hawkins
Senior Production Artist: Lora Puls
Production Artists: Shalana Fleetwood, John Rose,
Dana Vaughn, and Wendy Willets
Photography Stylists: Tiffany Huffman, Elizabeth
Lackey, and Janna Laughlin
Publishing Systems Administrator: Becky Riddle
Publishing Systems Assistants: Myra Means and Chri
Wertenberger

CREDITS

We want to extend a warm *thank you* to the
generous people who allowed us to photograph our
projects in their homes:
Bug Off!: Michael and Jodi Davis
Home On The Range: Mike and Ginger Townsend
Good Morning, Princess and **Ahoy, Mate!:**
Arch and Jennifer McIntosh
Wild Kingdom: Gordon and Pam Knetzer
The Magical Garden, Chicken Coop, and **Memory
Lane:** Shawn and Rhonda Fitz

Our sincere appreciation goes to photographers
Mark Mathews and Ken West of Peerless Photography,
Little Rock, Arkansas, and Jerry R. Davis of Jerry
Davis Photography, Little Rock, Arkansas, for their
excellent work.

To Wisconsin Technicolor LLC of Pewaukee,
Wisconsin, and Magna IV Color Imaging of Little Rock,
Arkansas, we say thank you for the superb color
reproduction and excellent pre-press preparation.

Copyright© 2000 by Leisure Arts, Inc., 5701 Ranch Drive, Little Rock, Arkansas 72223-9633. All rights reserved. Visit our Web site a
www.leisurearts.com. No part of this book may be reproduced in any form without the written permission of the publisher, except for brie
quotations in reviews appearing in magazines or newspapers. We have made every effort to ensure that these instructions are accurate ar
complete. We cannot, however, be responsible for human error, typographical mistakes, or variations in individual work. Made in the Unite
States of America.

International Standard Book Number 1-57486-203-0

10   9   8   7   6   5   4   3   2   1